The Puppy Diet

and Other Endearing Family Dog Tails

Beryl Jupiter

ISBN: 148028355X
ISBN-13: 9781480283558
Library of Congress Control Number: 2012921489
CreateSpace Independent Publishing Platform,
North Charleston, SC

Praise for The Puppy Diet

"It's a true "tail" of the ups and downs of pet ownership that is humorous, uplifting, and satisfying from start to finish."

—Jennifer, *CreateSpace* Editor

"It's a thorough depiction of dog ownership from the perspective of a candid matriarch. The author turned the physically exhausting process ... of raising a messy, mischievous puppy ... into a calculated weight-loss regime.

... Writing in a forthright, conversational voice, Jupiter doesn't shy away from the tough stuff ... expenses, training mishaps and the heartbreak of saying goodbye to a pet.

... It reads like a memoir, with nostalgic portraits of each of her dogs. It's hard not to smile when Jupiter decides not to cancel the morning newspaper because Tory enjoys retrieving it so much."

—*Kirkus Reviews*

"Unconditional love and unconditional fun, written with a sense of humor all dog owners will appreciate. Through life's ups and downs, puppy/dog companionship is priceless, and you might just lose a few pounds too."

—*Amazon* Customer 5-★ Review

"A must read for dog owners and dog lovers. Heart warming stories about dogs and their family."

—*Amazon* Customer 5-★ Review

Dedicated to Jesse,
my dear husband
and indispensable co-companion
to our six sporty dogs

Contents

Preface

As an occasional columnist for community newspapers for more than twenty years, I have often incorporated my personal voice and social experiences while intending to reflect universal themes to realistically resonate with readers.

Having written "The Puppy Diet" as an article for my hometown newspaper in suburban Boston, Massachusetts, I realized that the humorous topic might be an engaging entrée into an entire book of canine ownership issues. Dieting is ubiquitous and puppies are typically irresistible. I based the book mostly on my personal experiences of owning six sporty dogs but have hopefully presented common themes that are very relatable to many dog owners and animal lovers.

Humorously wagging my first tail/tale, I have presented my self-imposed diet plan devised to coincide with the anticipated high-energy expenditure of raising and socializing a boisterous English springer spaniel puppy. The book continues with many more chapters of comical and emotionally touching dog topics, such as dogs in bed, dogs as first children, dog training, restraining dogs, sports with dogs, chow time, pet sitting, dog grooming, sick dogs, and doggy empty nest.

I sincerely hope you enjoy reading this collection of canine concerns as much as I have loved living with our family dogs as well as writing about the delights and ordeals that dog ownership "en-tails."

Jupiter Family Chronology

Family Dogs

Lance (Sir Lancelot du Lac)
male Irish setter, 1973 to 1978

Brandy
female Irish setter, 1974 to 1980

Liza (Lydia's Lovely Liza)
female English springer spaniel, 1983 to 1998

Chelsea (Cricket's Charming Chelsea)
female English springer spaniel, 1992 to 2007

Harry (Wild about Harry)
male English springer spaniel, 1999 to present

Tory (Vivacious Victoria of Nonesuch)
female English springer spaniel, 2009 to present

Family People

Beryl Jupiter
wife, psychologist, dog co-owner, mother, writer

Jesse Jupiter
husband, orthopaedic/hand surgeon, dog co-owner, father

Stacy Jupiter
daughter, marine biologist, cat owner

Benjamin Jupiter
son, business career, dog owner

Chapter 1

The Puppy Diet

Hurry to get dressed, gate up rooms, step over gates, let my two dogs out, let dogs in, wipe eight paws, feed dogs separately, block dogs from eating each other's food, let dogs out again, toss tennis balls, walk dogs around the yard, clean up yard poops, remove rocks from puppy Tory's mouth, keep towels and clothes and shoes from Tory's reach, chase after Tory to retrieve what she reached anyway, prevent entry into pantry, spray Bitter Apple to deter gnawing on kitchen furniture and cabinetry, wipe up accidents, spray Nature's Miracle to mask accident smells, referee ball and chewy ownership, fill water bowls, wipe up water spills, launder towels and dog bed covers, let dogs out again, collapse in hammock with one eye still on cavorting canines, repeat all of the above multiple times a day.

Just writing about my day was tiring. No wonder living it was utterly exhausting. But every exertion I made in the realm of raising a new puppy was cumulatively contributing to a welcome weight-loss regimen.

My most recent decision to bring a new puppy home was not made lightly. First-time puppy owners may be blissfully oblivious to the requisite time and energy to socialize the adorable beast into a compatible household companion. But as a longtime dog owner of active sporting dogs, I am all too acquainted with the surprisingly large amount of care and attention that a young canine demands as well as the shocking amount of mess and destruction that such a furry bundle of joy inevitably creates.

With the acquisition of our family's third English springer spaniel when I was in my late forties, I was enmeshed 24/7 with intensive puppy socialization. Constantly interrupted to take puppy Harry outside for optimal house training or to extract him from some naughty behavior within the house, I hardly had a chance to finish a meal. I was inadvertently eating less than usual and was physically active to the point of exhaustion. I could not possibly imagine how I would ever have the patience and strength to raise another puppy at some later stage of my life.

Fast-forward eight years. That's how much older I was when our second springer Chelsea died of old age in 2007, leaving Harry a somewhat lonely only dog. But, exhausted from aging canine care, I was not in any hurry to replace Chelsea. The urination accidents of our senior dog had increased exponentially. I had to tiptoe through our kitchen every morning to avoid overnight puddles. A mop was always in the ready position throughout the day. Even as I recuperated from compassionate Chelsea care, I still vividly remembered the exhausting ordeal of raising Harry, which would undoubtedly resurface as a nightmarish *déjà vu* in the presence of a newly arriving puppy.

But after two years as a one-dog family, it finally seemed time to add another dog into the Jupiter family constellation. Not that I had in any way forgotten the prior complications of puppy rearing, but this time I had a plan. I would work the shortened eating time and exhausting physical activity to my advantage.

I created my own puppy diet!

Knowing I would be in the same continuous movement predicament as previously experienced, I began a weight-loss regimen to coincide with acquiring our fourth English springer spaniel. And the diet worked like a charm, given the combination of reduced caloric intake and exceedingly more physical activity than I would ever choose to exert without a damn good reason.

Of course, I had to figure out what food to eat on my puppy diet. Interrupted meals are not an optimal calorie reduction plan and could potentially result in ravenous between-meal snacking. The irony of middle age is that I have been eating more healthy foods in less quantity than at any other time of my life but still have a tendency to gain weight—totally unfair and especially frustrating.

My most successful attempts at dieting in adulthood were with Diet Center® (a well-balanced, low-calorie diet) and with the South Beach® diet (maximizing healthy carbs and minimizing fats). But eventually, over time, the diet gets old, my stick-to-it-iveness diminishes, and the weight creeps back up. Case in point: the celebrity diet story about actress Kirstie Alley, the glamorous poster pinup for Jenny Craig® who quickly regained her entire, well-touted seventy-five-pound weight loss. But when Kirstie subsequently competed on the television show *Dancing with the*

Stars, she expended so much physical energy that she lost the weight again.

About the same time as my puppy acquisition, a diet study reported in the *New England Journal of Medicine* (February, 2009) attracted much attention in national news media. Overweight adults were randomly assigned to diets that varied food intake of fats, proteins, and carbohydrates. Popular diets like Atkins had emphasized avoiding carbohydrates and eating predominantly protein and fats. Other diets had recommended avoiding fats, limiting proteins, and/or eating more carbs. This study sought to determine whether specific food types were optimal for weight loss.

What particularly impressed me were the findings: the types of foods ingested had no bearing whatsoever on weight loss. But there were three factors that made a significant difference: total caloric intake, amount of exercise, and a support system.

So I decided to devise my own low-calorie diet based on what worked for me in the past, add additional exercise to my daily routine, and talk often to diet-oriented, weight-loss-challenged friends about dieting concerns (my personal support system). And to keep myself honest and on track, I began a food journal, recording absolutely everything that I put in my mouth, and calculating calories by weighing and measuring all foods, with the help of a new food scale and a helpful website called thecaloriecounter.com.

And speaking of weighing, I made sure to weigh myself too, even though the first diet day on my bathroom scale was always the most daunting. But I talked myself into the frightening feat, rationalizing that I wouldn't know how much I'd really lost if I didn't climb on the scary scale at the onset of my diet. So I did it, didn't like the number, resolved to lower it, and continued to weigh myself daily, even after the occasional days of eating excess. If you fall off the horse, you have to get right back in the saddle. The same applies to the diet and the scale.

I did not starve myself, not even close. I ate three meals a day and between-meal snacks of mostly healthy, low-calorie foods in smaller portions than usual.

Meanwhile, my life was a continuous "puppercise." I was in constant motion from earlier in the morning than I cared to be awake. But I wasn't complaining. I was on the fast track to weight loss while enjoying my adorable puppy at her cutest, albeit most demanding, stage of life. Tory was the sweetest wiggly bundle of soft, silky fur, who looked up at me adoringly with her shiny brown puppy eyes and tickled me with her warm, damp puppy-tongue kisses (when she wasn't biting me, however affectionately, with her wound-inflicting puppy sharp teeth).

In the first month that I had Tory, I lost about ten pounds and she gained about the same amount. Finally a lost-and-found scenario that I could get excited about compared to vacations when my husband tended to lose weight while I seemed to find Jesse's pounds attached me.

Tory would not be a puppy forever. I presumed I wouldn't be thin forever. But I greatly enjoyed both coinciding conditions for as long as they lasted. And surprising even to me, a significant weight loss lasted almost two years as I ramped up my physical activity with the demands of our boisterous puppy. Furthermore, additional exertions were unexpectedly necessitated to care for poor Harry who was beset by a nasty series of ailments around the same time period.

Over time and with training, maturing Tory became less physically demanding. And having bounded back from knee surgery and other acutely incapacitating maladies, Harry was released from restrictions that required close monitoring. So, with less dog-driven tasks, returning pounds gradually accumulated on the slender me that was too good to last. But, I did not fully return to my puffy pre-Tory body.

That's why I tolerate the dirtier jobs of dog ownership. I wipe eight paws multiple times a day for my fickle Fidos who always want to come inside seemingly moments after they've begged to go out. They're "always on the wrong side of the door," per the apt expression I learned from a similarly exasperated dog-owner friend. I repeatedly stoop to scoop the plentiful poops that litter our property, even though I could farm out the nasty task to Doody Calls on a regular basis. But from my diet-conscious perspective, whether I am cleaning dogs or the lawn, I am simultaneously burning off copious calories.

(See Appendix for my personal dieting choices for the Puppy Diet, with hints and suggestions.)

Chapter 2

Dogs in Bed

I am not at all sure how it all got started. But Lance was our first dog that we raised from a puppy. Jesse and I had been married for two years when we moved from the Northeast to an Indian reservation (his idea) in the Arizona desert (sort of my idea, lots closer to civilization than his preferred choices of Montana or Alaska). On our driving trip out west in 1973, intermittently camping (Jesse's preference) and staying at motor inns (guess whose preference?), we noticed lots of people hiking with sporty dogs running at their heels. How cool was that! Admittedly, my prior hiking experiences were primarily nature walks (often under protest) at overnight camp in the Pocono Mountains. And the family dogs of my youth pretty much stayed put at our house except for necessary outings around our yard.

The dogs that especially caught my eye as we proceeded west were stately Irish setters, with their shiny auburn fringe and flapping long ears. So, shortly after arriving on the Gila River Indian Reservation, I cruised the *Arizona Republic* classified dog ads until I found an Irish setter litter listing in the Phoenix area. That was about forty miles north of our new homestead in Sacaton where Jesse had signed on as general medical officer in the Indian Health Service after completing medical school and a year of internship. While I thought Irish setters were extraordinarily handsome, I found the puppies to be incredibly adorable. And I was generally gaga over our little Sir Lancelot du Lac, named for the valorous French knight of Camelot, but always called more simply Lance.

Before long the little fellow was a rip-roaring bundle of energy and an uncontained whirlwind of blissful devastation. The covers of our prized LP (that's how long ago that was) collection, neatly lined up against a wall, were all gnawed off at the corners. And the enthusiastic tail wagging of our frisky Fido, pretty much at cocktail table height, whisked many tabletop items to their ultimate demise. The worst case was the smashing of an ancient Hohokam pottery dish unearthed at a local construction site and gifted to Jesse by an appreciative Pima Indian friend. We still bemoan the loss to this day when we encounter similar pottery displayed at Native American museums and historical sites.

Meanwhile, once Lance was house-trained, we ignorantly began to include the cuddly canine, who was much more adorable asleep than active, into our bed at night. And in our early married years we just had a double bed. What were we thinking? Not only do male Irish setters grow quite large, but Lance also had a habit of nosing his head right up to our pillows between our heads. So there were three in the bed, and no little one said, "Roll over." It was just a tight squeeze.

Well, if one Irish setter was so much fun, how much more fun would two be, I wondered. So after only one year of dog ownership, I once again perused the *Republic's* dog ads for Irish setter litters. Not particularly discriminating, I bought another setter pup from the first Phoenix area breeder I read about and visited. Thus came home Brandy, a cute pedigreed pup but high-pitched little girl dog (avoiding the "bitch" term due to its unfortunately pejorative association) to befriend us and virile Lance. Before too long, and without realizing the long-term implications, we had two Irish setters sharing our overcrowded double bed.

And the reality is that once you invite dogs into your bed, they do not consider the bed yours. From their canine perspective, the bed is now theirs. You are in their way, not at all vice versa.

Squeezing all of us into bed was awkward, but we were young and flexible, both physically and mentally. When we moved after two years on the reservation with our Irish setters to the woodsy suburbs of the Boston area, the setters were still sleeping with us. Even though we bought our first queen-size bed for our Wellesley starter home, it was hardly more spacious, since by then I was pregnant. But I was highly discouraging of any dog noses or butts near my face and not averse to kicking canines to the foot of the bed, where they could curl up less intrusively.

Unfortunately, with dogs in the bed also came the insects that latched onto our canines. And that was before the widespread use of topical flea and tick deterrent. How disconcerting to detect a stealthy creepy crawler in the bedding or somewhere on our human bodies—or worse yet, to find a little bloodsucker already firmly attached.

We eventually lost Lance and Brandy to health problems and moving and were dog-less for some of the early years of our children's lives. But when we bought our children's first family dog, when Stacy was seven and Benjy was five, I pronounced that I had enough of dogs in my bed. So while Lydia's (her mother) Lovely Liza, our first English springer spaniel, was banned from the master bed, she often found a comfy mattress and inviting warm body with either of our children. Or she commonly curled up on the floor by our bed on a turned-down bedspread.

Over the years, our beloved Liza developed a habit of not settling down for the night until all her charges were home and tucked in. Reminiscent of the nursemaid dog Nana of *Peter Pan* fame, Liza would stake herself out on the staircase landing until each of us made our way to bed for the night, no matter how late. And considering Jesse's late-night surgeon's hours and eventually our teenagers' weekend outings, it was often very late. But only then would Liza choose her ultimate sleeping quarters for the evening.

Preventing a dog from jumping in bed requires constant vigilance, and apparently I'd run out of it by the time we added our second springer Cricket's (her mother) Charming Chelsea to the family. Even though Liza had been well trained to sleep next to, not on our bed, I had lost the patience to train Chelsea to stay out of the bed. However, I insisted on one important rule: no jumping up until the bedspread was turned down. At least I kept some semblance of cleanliness, as sheets and blankets can be washed much more easily than bedspreads and comforters. So Liza kept sleeping with the kids or at the foot of our bed, while Chelsea had her pick of beds, including ours. I dealt with it.

After our wonderful family dog Liza died at almost fifteen years old, I needed a full year to recuperate from caring for an aging, Alzheimer's-like pooch. About then we were apprised of a litter of English springer spaniels while vacationing on Martha's Vineyard with seven-year-old Chelsea. Her presence encouraged the house gardener to inform us of the litter at Heather Gardens Nursery. I was naturally inclined to visit the pups but nevertheless recognized how adorably seductive I would find them. So when I didn't rush to check them out, Jesse's sister Vivian, vacationing with us then, eventually asked, "What are you waiting for? Let's go see the puppies." I knew what I was waiting for. I was avoiding the inevitable. I could predict my reaction. One visit and there'd be no turning back. I would be puppy-hooked.

The biggest decision was not whether to buy one of the litter but rather to how to select one of the seven adorable furry bundles. My decision was mercifully narrowed by my interest in obtaining a male (opposite of Chelsea) of liver and white color (same as Liza and Chelsea). Three of the litter met my criteria. And of those three, the biggest pup of the entire litter, originally dubbed Bruno, was already taken. The puppy with the wide white blaze on his forehead captivated me.

So I brought Wild about Harry home, at only six weeks old, the first to leave the litter. Although planning to release the puppies at seven weeks, Heather allowed me to take our choice sooner due to the potential inconvenience of making a return car ferry trip to the Vineyard. I felt like quite a villain tearing Harry away from his birth family. And he was vocally distraught in the cardboard pet carrier they provided for car transport home. As I was driving alone, I eventually made a "nest" for Harry in the passenger seat of our Isuzu Rodeo, which he thankfully found much more to his liking. But when I needed a bathroom break awaiting off-island ferry departure, I had to take little Harry with me to the Vineyard Haven ferry building restroom. While holding him carefully and awkwardly, I managed my personal business in the stall.

Once home, I initially provided Harry an appropriately sized training crate, for both daytime containment and overnight bedtime. Time-limited day crating was fairly successful for house training and protecting interior decor from potential puppy destruction. But Harry remained vocally distressed in his crated nighttime habitat, inexplicably isolated from his customary cozy pile of warm doggy bodies. So we agonized till he cried himself to sleep. But as a young pup, Harry didn't make it through the night. He usually woke up after several hours, crying for an outing—just like a baby, and of course, he was a baby. Either Jesse or I would release him from the crate, take him outside to take care of his business, and then return him to the crate. Quite distressingly, the pitiful crying would resume, penetrating the bathroom walls where I sequestered the crate and piercing our ears and hearts. Not that I was hard-hearted, but I preferred to stick to the training plan, assuming Harry would eventually go along with the program. However, at about four months old, Harry was still making us too aware of his mid-night loneliness. One night Jesse had enough. Having attended to the exhausting middle-of-the-night outing, Jesse did not return Harry to his crate. Despite my protests, Jesse plopped our plaintive pooch in the middle of our bed. You never heard, or actually didn't hear, a quieter puppy. He was back to sleep instantaneously.

From then on, as far as Harry was concerned, our bed was his bed. He never had an accident in our bed, which was something I initially feared. And he no longer awoke in the middle of the night. All Harry wanted was to cuddle up with a pile of warm bodies, and that was exactly what Jesse, Chelsea, and I provided.

With all our dogs, the puppies did not have the run of the house. So puppy Harry's daytime freedom was limited to the tile floor of our kitchen and breakfast area, where occasional accidents could be most thoroughly cleaned and sanitized. And since our carpeted bedroom is accessed from the kitchen, I kept our bedroom door closed. Once Harry claimed our bed as his, however, he would camp out by the bedroom door from about eight p.m. on, with a look on his face that seemed to say, "I am sleepy. I want to go to bed. Let me in that room. My bed is behind that door. What are you waiting for?" As always, there were mounds of dog beds scattered in the kitchen/breakfast area, but when it came to evening bedtime, Harry anxiously awaited the master bed.

And once maturing Harry had open access to the bedroom, he had to learn, like Chelsea before him, that jumping on top of the bed was only allowed when the bedspread was pulled down for the night. Surprisingly, all it took were a few loud and stern "No's" to the disallowed leap and repetitions of "Wait" until I removed the spread followed by "OK" when the bed was ready for dog (and people) entry to imprint the desired behavior. So once Harry was allowed free bedroom entry, we often found him waiting impatiently at the side of the bed when he was personally ready for bedtime but the spread was still in place.

So what happened to me? Wasn't I that person who insisted, after bedding down with two Irish setters, that I was done with dogs in my bed? Almost twenty years later I was again sharing my bed with two dogs! I just kept insisting that I have first priority to my pillows and the head of my bed and that I be able to straighten my legs. And I would not tolerate noses or butts in my face. Yet when the television remote control is missing, it usually is buried underneath a dog.

Chelsea often had the good sense to jump out of our bed at night due to overcrowding. So I always kept a dog bed in our bedroom floor for Chelsea's bedding options. Harry, however, has been and continues to be a steady fixture in our bed since Jesse's first plopping him there during his puppyhood.

After Chelsea died of old age, we temporarily had ample stretching room in bed for many months of one-dog nights. Almost two years elapsed until I considered becoming a two-dog family again. But what breed this time? Fleeting thoughts of another Irish setter were dismissed. Perhaps the compact Australian shepherd, of similar size, intelligence, and energy to our springers. And for quite some time, I had been much attracted to the fluffy, bear-like Bernese mountain dog. But I was reluctant to acquire such a large dog, especially with my seeming inability to ban puppy pack mates from our bed.

So as I once again searched for familiar English springers, I fortunately found an adorable litter of tricolored spaniels within a reasonable travel radius. And unexpectedly, Vivacious Victoria, being black, white, and tan, has a striking similarity of markings to a Bernese mountain dog. Compared to our prior three springers, Tory is more bear cub-like, with a chunkier build and thicker fur. Endearingly, I call her my "mini-Bernie."

Just like Harry, however, puppy Tory was quite distraught at her nighttime separation from the family in her lonely crate and reminiscently vocalized her distress in lengthy fits of sorrowful whimpering and whining. While I tried to prolong the crate training, Jesse began wearing his Bose noise-cancelling earphones to bed. The earphones are reasonably effective for optimal airplane music listening or movie viewing but do not completely drown out heart-wrenching cries of distressed babies on planes or puppies in-house.

So having experienced Harry's settling down so peacefully when installed in our bed, Jesse tried the same with Tory—at an even earlier age and despite my repeat protestations. Not surprisingly, three-month-old Tory was similarly thrilled to snuggle up with the rest of her new family in our comfy bed, minimizing her nighttime distress. I was initially worried, however, about her rousing in the night and having immediate needs that would not wait till we got her outside.

Fortunately, we had no accidents in bed. And early on, Tory feared jumping off our highly piled box spring and mattress, so there was no night wandering. All the same, I had to rush through my own early morning necessities to ensure Tory's getting out of bed in a timely manner or remove her, under protest, to her crate for several minutes until I was ready for her first morning outing.

The next concern came when Tory lost her fear of hopping off the bed, which led to mid-night wandering. While I was most concerned with uncontrolled elimination, more problematic was her making chew toys of TV remotes and throw rugs while we slept oblivious to her destructive activities.

So to date we generally have two dogs sleeping in our bed. For thirteen years Harry has claimed our bed as his nighttime crash pad and has no inclination to do otherwise. He continues to wait patiently bedside until the spread is removed and he is permitted to hop on top. However, his hop has lost its original pop. To spring upon our thick pillow top mattress at his advancing age and hobbled by a rear-leg anterior cruciate ligament tear, Harry has taught himself to take a running start to mount the mattress. Once bedded down, Harry is not easily discouraged from his summit, regardless of my shoving and kicking to claim my rightful few feet of mattress solace.

When puppy Tory also claimed our bed for nighttime sleep, she was not initially able to jump on top of the oversized combo of box spring and pillow top mattress. Our young springer spaniel would beg to be lifted with her front legs leaning on the bedding until one of us hoisted her up. That suited me fine until she learned she could jump off the bed, which she repeatedly did throughout the night. She seemed to find various reasons to hop out of bed while we slept: for a drink, to get a toy, or to just spread out for more room on the floor, as Chelsea had done before her. The problem was the sleep-disrupting requests for re-entry to the sleeping shrine as she whined at bedside, which was certainly not conducive to a good night's sleep for the bed's human occupants.

Our chunkiest springer seemed delayed in developing her "spring." By the time spring-less Tory was eight months old, Jesse was frustrated enough by sleep "interruptus" that he finally used significant hand-waving motions to get Tory to leap onto the bed by herself. That solved one problem but created another. Tory began to jump up indiscriminately, regardless of the presence of the decorative bedspread. Training for bed-jumping restraint was my job, which took considerable scolding and dragging Tory off the bed until she understood when bed entry was and was not allowed. Now Tory is relatively patient as she sits with eager anticipation through our spread and excess pillow removing activities until the bed is considered dog-permissible.

Not long after Tory learned to leap into bed on her own, we had a new problem with bed entry and exit. This situation involved Harry who required surgery on his left rear leg for the increasingly debilitating tear of his ACL, or anterior cruciate ligament (but technically known in dogs as CCL, or cranial cruciate ligament). For optimal healing, post-op activities were severely restricted, and that certainly included jumping on or off the bed. If teaching an old dog new tricks is difficult, it's even harder to teach the cessation of old tricks. Despite trying to anticipate Harry's inclination to jump, we were not always fast enough to grab and assist him.

With my concern for Harry's recuperation overriding my concern for attractive bedroom décor, I reluctantly ordered a new piece of furniture. The portable three-step, beige-carpeted staircase was surprisingly less ugly than I had anticipated. And with some insistent retraining, we managed to encourage Harry to walk up the stairs into bed. Getting Harry to descend by steps was more challenging, as he impatiently wanted to jump out of bed as soon as early-rising Jesse got up. At least Harry's front legs seemed to hit the floor first when leaping off, hopefully having taken the brunt of pressure off the operated rear leg.

Once fully recuperated after two months of post-op physical restrictions (as hard on me as on Harry due to my being the restrictions supervisor), aging Harry has never reverted to leaping onto our bed again. Throughout the day the steps are kept unobtrusively against a bedroom wall and moved bedside only after decorative bedspread and pillows are removed at night. Then Harry gently and appreciatively climbs his "stairway to heaven." And most of the time, he also exits by stair steps, gingerly descending and optimally minimizing rear leg pounding and possible repeat ligament rupture.

As much as I loved my dogs and tolerated their presence in my bed, there was not much room for me. I found myself increasingly being nudged to the edge of the mattress or unable to fully extend my cramp-prone legs. If I temporarily departed from bed in the middle of the night, I commonly returned to find Tory stubbornly snuggled in my vacated space. Drowsy with sleep, I was not pleased to tussle with an immoveable mutt.

So after thirty-five years of sleeping in our queen-size home bed with my husband, our son in his younger years, and our assortment of pets (which included a cat that sometimes joined the slumber party during our one-dog family interludes), I decided we needed a king-size bed. After waiting for Tory to outgrow her most destructive puppy stage and searching for the best bed frame accompaniment to the rest of our room's furniture, I am thrilled with the more spacious sleeping environment that we now call bedtime. I can't even imagine how we all fit in queen-size sleeping quarters when I observe our former relatively compact bed relocated into our guest room. Admittedly, I still get squeezed to one edge of our much bigger bed. But at least there's a lot more room to stretch my legs and nudge or kick the dogs out of my personal space.

Space in bed, however, is not the only problem created by two dogs. Another is cleanliness. Jesse often lets them out in the middle of the night and usually early in the morning before he leaves for work. Then both dogs return to bed with me, with eight feet that are rarely wiped fully clean. As a result, the extra top sheet over our blanket or comforter requires laundering every couple of days. I adore the months of frozen ground and snow cover when very little dirt adheres to their paws. Unfortunately, winter is followed by spring thaw and muddy-paw season.

Tory, our tricolored springer, presented yet another problem. She prodigiously shed more puppy hair than any of our other dogs as she grew her adult coat of fur. Every morning I was confronted by a dander of black hairs all over the top sheet and the decision to launder or wait one more day. Thankfully, Jesse and I are not allergic.

But admittedly, mornings are sometimes a problem when the dogs want to arise before I am ready to awaken. Usually Jesse lets them out early so they do not have urgent needs upon my arising. But if Harry hears or smells some animal outside, he may be anxious to check it out. Or if Tory hears the newspaper vehicle, she rustles our bedroom shades to confirm the delivery and impatiently requests to retrieve the paper.

These days my early-rising husband is typically also early to bed—much earlier than I am interested in bedding down for the night. As soon as Jesse strips off the decorative bedding, Tory impatiently springs into bed and contentedly curls into her nighttime crash position. With Jesse's also arranging the portable staircase bedside, Harry may make a brief visit to the communal sleeping quarters. But my loyal older dog will shortly descend bedtime heaven to spend most of the evening resting in my office, patiently awaiting my eventual bedding down for the night, reminiscent of "Nana" Liza.

As much as we acquiesce to dogs in our bed, we rationally exclude them when the bedroom activity is not sleep. Cavorting canines are not included in our intimate marital interludes, although I am sure our pets would love to playfully participate in nuzzling and corporeal intertwining. While canine cuddling at bedtime is allowed, we draw the line at furry sexual *menage à trois* or *quatre.* As the exclusionary bedroom door is closed and gated, we offer compensatory chew flips to temporarily preoccupy our inexplicably banished pups.

But generally our dogs delightedly share our comfortable human bed. Although, I admittedly wonder why we tolerate bed rest disturbances and limited stretching space while sullied by dirt, hair, and occasional creepy crawlers. Our house is not so cold that we require a two-dog night. The trade-off for us, I suppose, must be the endearing sneaky snuggling of a warm, fuzzy muzzle.

Harry and Tory napping with Jesse

Chapter 3

First Children

Admittedly, our Irish setters were our first children. But honestly, they had to take a back seat when we added human children to our family.

As we prepared for our first child, we wondered how Lance and Brandy would behave with a baby in the house. Jesse and I knew our parents were concerned about how we would introduce our baby to our two large dogs.

Shortly after bringing baby Stacy home, we were expecting a family gathering to meet our newborn. Jesse and I were sitting together in Stacy's room and in came Lance. He pawed through the air to say hello and swiped Stacy lightly on her face, creating a glaring (from our perspective) red mark on her cheek. Baby's skin is really sensitive. But how were we going to explain the "gash" to the relatives? Fortunately, it faded enough to be hardly noticeable by the time they arrived.

When Stacy was a year old, I went to graduate school. Mornings were always hectic as I got her ready to take to family day care. One day I hurriedly refreshed the dog water and food on the porch, and the kitchen door accidentally closed and locked behind me. I was out, and toddler Stacy was in and so were two large circulating setters. I hurried to my neighbors' house to call the police and returned to worriedly watch their interaction through the window. Fortunately, no harm came to Stacy as she meandered around the kitchen with the dogs until the police arrived and easily accessed my house through a first-floor window. Police would make very good burglars.

When we bought our house in Wellesley, a town with no leash law at the time, we were still concerned how neighbors might feel about our two big dogs. So we immediately installed a five-foot wooden fence in the backyard to contain them. Unfortunately, the more we tried to keep them in, the more they wanted out. And they dug holes to try to escape or just to see what was on the other side. Eventually, when I was at home, I just let them out of the fenced yard to minimize the excavating. Lance seemed to have wanderlust. I think Brandy would have been perfectly content to stay home, but she followed after Lance.

We lived just a few blocks from the commercial area of Wellesley Hills with grocery stores, take-out shops, and restaurants, so that's where they tended to go—basically anywhere that someone would give them a handout. We even heard that they would try to follow friendly people onto the public bus. On occasion I was called by the Wellesley Fire Department, informing me that our unsettled setters had found their way to the firehouse. That was particularly worrisome because they had to cross a busy double-lane highway to get there. Sometimes Fire Chief Duddy, who was my house painter in his other day job, would kindly drive the dogs back to my house. Our Irish setters looked just as comfortable as Dalmatians riding fire truck shotgun.

By the time we had a second baby, Lance was five years old but had been suffering with systemic dermatitis for years. Despite repeated steroid injections, oral meds, and topical ointments, his condition was barely amenable to treatment. We were always admonishing him to quit biting himself and were quite distressed by his raw, bald, and sore-covered skin patches. Although Lance was my first "child," I felt we could no longer keep him and thought we should give him away for adoption. It was not an easy decision for us and was made worse when we were informed that no one would adopt a dog with his skin problems. So Jesse had the sorry task to bring Lance to Angell Memorial Hospital to be euthanized. It didn't help any that another pet owner in the waiting area complimented Jesse on his handsome dog. I still feel guilt pangs in recalling our conflicted decision to part with Lance.

That left us with two kids and one dog, our smaller, more manageable female setter. As a toddler and preschooler, Stacy often complained, "Brandy's bothering me," and would ask me to remove our nosy dog from whatever she was doing. When we made plans to leave Wellesley for Jesse's orthopaedic and hand surgery fellowship training, we listed our house for rent for a year with intentions to return to the Boston area. Initially I hadn't figured out what we'd be doing with Brandy, as we were going to Switzerland followed by Louisville, Kentucky. When a recently divorced man arranged to rent our house, I jokingly asked him if he'd like to rent our dog as well, and to my surprise, he wanted to keep Brandy too. She would be good company for him and an additional incentive for his son to visit, he said.

As is often said, absence makes the heart grow fonder. Four year-old Stacy loved to draw, and more and more her absent dog Brandy was lovingly featured in her drawings. Brandy wasn't bothering her anymore from afar.

Meanwhile, the longer we were away, Brandy was endearing herself to our tenant. After several months, Ed wrote to me, in traditional mail of 1980 vintage, with a special request. Having become very attached to Brandy, he asked if he could keep her even after we returned.

Jesse left the decision about Brandy to me. Intensely involved in his surgical training, he had minimal availability for dog care. Meanwhile, our young children were consuming most of my time and energy, leaving me much less inclined to dog parenting than during the pre-children stage of my life. So I told Ed, by return handwritten note, that he could keep Brandy. The more difficult task was to diplomatically inform Stacy that we would no longer own the dog whose beloved qualities had greatly increased in absentia. Ed was lonely, I explained, because of the change in his family, and he needed Brandy for company more than we did now. Our precocious four year-old was surprisingly understanding.

Irish setters were our first dogs and first children. I still love looking at their adorable puppy pictures. We had them from 1973 to 1979. They were highly energetic and quite a handful, but they taught me a lot about taking care of, cleaning up after, and being responsible for those other than myself. They were excellent practice for real human children.

Chapter 4

Fenced In

Family dogs live in our homes, but they usually want to and need to go outside—of course, to relieve themselves, but also to exercise, to smell the world, to meet other furry friends, and generally to frolic around in the great outdoors. We have to organize our world for all of that to happen by devoting time and restraints to ensure safe and sufficient outings for our pets.

I knew all that when I acquiesced to my teenage son's request to get a puppy. I knew because we already had a dog—Liza, a wonderful, friendly, nine-year-old English springer spaniel. With no town leash law at that time, Liza had become a free-spirited pooch who managed her own outings, independently roamed our neighborhood, and reliably returned home to her much-loved people family every day. Even though my son promised to help with the new pup, I agreed to purchase darling Chelsea, an adorable miniature Liza, knowing full well who really would be out at all hours of the day and in all kinds of weather.

And walk we did, Chelsea and I, morning, noon, and night, and many intervals in between, through a winter of shovel-high snow drifts, frostbite-inducing wind chills, and almost insurmountable walls of snowplow creation. Foolishly, I did not particularly consider the weather when we brought Chelsea home in November. It was just my bad luck that the 1992-1993 winter season turned out be Boston's third snowiest on record to that date, piling up a whopping snowfall total of eighty-four inches (Source: www.noaa.gov). And in our western suburb, located about fifteen miles inland, snow totals always surpassed official Boston measures taken harborside at Logan Airport.

While Chelsea's outings were a challenge, I optimistically focused on the positive. Liza got more quality time outside with me too. I met many neighbors, introduced to me by Liza. My long johns and woolen outerwear got excellent use. And of most benefit, I never gained my usual five pounds of winter weight. I was on a puppy diet without my even recognizing it.

However, with spring's thaw and warmer temps, I hoped I could leave a maturing Chelsea outside on her own occasionally. So I tried tying my energetic pup to Liza's old fifty-foot run, supposedly engineered to be a semi-adequate walk substitute. But apparently not for Chelsea, who rarely moved from the spot where she was hooked, and constantly vocalized, "Bark, bark [come get me], bark, bark [I'm waiting], bark, bark [I'm lonely], bark, bark, [where are you?] bark, bark, bark ..." No "business" done and no exercise, except for the vocal chords.

I hoped Chelsea could eventually roam free like Liza, so I started to let her loose when I was in the yard. I just had to yell, "Chelsea, good girl," every fifteen seconds to make sure she stayed in earshot. But if a neighbor or jogger passed by, the pup bolted, as I held my breath and prayed vigorously for no vehicular traffic.

So how did Liza become a minimally wandering and reliably returning, street-wise spaniel, the cheerful companion of neighborhood walkers and infants in strollers? Most likely by neglect, as I was more preoccupied with my young children and busy working-mother life.

My long-repressed memories of Liza's youthful years of wanderlust gradually resurfaced: my worriedly cruising the neighborhood in search of my wayward woofer; spending hours one Halloween night trying to locate our missing spaniel; getting calls from concerned strangers near major thoroughfares or annoyed counselors at the nearby day camp whose little campers were literally bowled over by our over-friendly hound; or being greeted by a returning mud-caked explorer, disgustingly blackened from nose to tail.

Seemingly, Liza's enviable behavior evolved mostly from maturational mellowing (hers, not mine). But I couldn't imagine reliving Liza's youth through Chelsea and regularly worrying about a motor accident or unexplained disappearance. Yet I was not inclined to install traditional visible fencing, which would impinge on the openness of our property. And my prior experience trying to contain our Irish setters within a wooden fenced yard had less than optimal results, as our confined canines destroyed the lawn in their exhaustive attempts to dig their way out.

Hence my call to the purveyors of the Invisible Fence®. Even before the company's sales associate visited me, I had already sold myself on the idea of an electronic dog containment system with truly no visible barriers. Wearing an electrical receiving collar, an untethered dog can go out unattended. She will stay within her property to avoid an electric shock emanating from a wire buried around the perimeter. Although not an inexpensive device, it was actually less costly than traditional wooden fencing.

But would it be heartless to wire Chelsea to a shock deterrent? When offered the opportunity to feel the electrical charge, I felt obligated to experience it. Hesitantly I touched the activated collar prongs and felt a sensation like a strong static electricity shock (fairly similar to the frequent experience in our heated house's dry atmosphere throughout severe New England winters). Not too cruel, I reasoned, if it prevented a more tragic incident.

Actually, prewarned by a buzzing sound emanating eight feet from the buried wire and trained by flags as visual cues to the invisible boundary, Chelsea was rarely shocked. She stayed well within our perimeter, un-tempted to breech the boundary to follow joggers, bikers, other dogs, or even Liza (who we never wired since she had already become such an adept and reliable neighborhood wanderer).

As a cheerful one-year-old, Chelsea spent more time outside with Liza on our property. She got more exercise and was less rowdy in the house. But I got out less and would have to find another way to keep off the winter weight. Admittedly, our beds of impatiens took a beating, but I determined optimal planting placement for the following spring to avoid major dog trampling areas.

Warned that a turned-on television could activate the IF receiver of mid-1990s vintage, we almost always removed Chelsea's collar in the house. But unfortunately for Chelsea, we learned the hard way that the concern was valid. Wearing the collar I had forgotten to remove indoors, Chelsea walked close to our thirty-six-inch Mitsubishi TV that was considered quite large for that era. When I heard her unusually high-pitched yelp, I belatedly and remorsefully removed the collar. Another time I got my own test of the warning as I was holding onto the collar while walking close to a television. Zap! I dropped the collar like a hot potato.

Those were accidents. But inexplicably our son's teenage friend Jeremy intentionally donned Chelsea's collar and ran through the Invisible Fence perimeter. Relaying this incident to me, amid wails of laughter, Ben said it was not a pretty sight. While this fence concept worked great for a dog, I didn't expect it to contain a teenager, but it might have just slowed him down.

When we moved around the corner to a different house when Chelsea was about five years old, we did not initially install an Invisible Fence. I had to watch out for fourteen-year-old Liza anyway, who had never been trained to the IF system. And Alzheimer's-like Liza, who had had the run of the neighborhood her entire life, might be inclined to return to our old house, which was only three-quarters of a mile away by roads, even less if cutting through backyards.

Chelsea was not initially rushing off our new property anyway. It seemed what she had learned by her Invisible Fence training was to not stray too far from her house. When aging Liza died the next year, Chelsea was on her own but still very much self-confined to our property.

However, when new next-door neighbors moved in, they often lovingly greeted Chelsea outside, which inspired her wandering next door for more friendly neighborhood interaction. And that little bit of wandering led to more. Although we had moved to a very quiet, private street, problems developed in leaving Chelsea out by herself.

A summer concern, which had also developed with Liza's wanderings, was the nearby children's day camp. Although some children were excited to meet a cheerful visiting canine, others were petrified by a jumpy dog. Like Liza before her, we had several episodes of camp counselors' tying up Chelsea and calling me to retrieve her.

Another major problem that developed due to off-property exploration was Chelsea's attraction to the swampy areas nearby. She would return home on her own, but covered in black boggy goop, which would require an immediate bathing. Knowing what was coming, Chelsea tried to avoid my catching her. To get her mud-caked body near enough for me to leash her, I had to tempt her with an outstretched hot dog.

Chelsea's short-lived independence would have to be curbed. I arranged to have the Invisible Fence installed at our new home. Chelsea quickly trained to her new perimeters due to prior familiarity with the IF system.

Chelsea was an only dog for fifteen months by the time we brought puppy Harry home. As a puppy, Harry pretty much followed Chelsea around so there was little chance of him wandering away on his own. Nevertheless, I checked with the Invisible Fence® company about when to train Harry to the fence. They recommended at six months old. So, I conscientiously arranged his training at their suggested age, even though it was January.

The training began with re-flagging the perimeter and Harry's being fitted with a signal collar. At first the dog hears a distinctive tone as he approaches the perimeter and sees the flags, pairing the auditory and visual stimuli. The metal prongs of the signal collar are initially covered with rubber so no shock is felt. But after several days, the rubber cover is removed. As the dog is allowed to wander close to the perimeter, he experiences a shock. Learning occurs through the conditioned pairing of the flag, tone, and shock. Once associated with the aversive shock, the flags and tone quickly become sufficient warnings about advancing further.

Harry was a very sensitive young pup about lots of learning experiences. He seemed very smart right from the start, learned quickly, and liked to follow a routine. When he experienced his first Invisible Fence shock, he totally freaked out, ran back to our deck, and refused to step off the deck of his own volition. Poor little Harry! He was so distressed. And I felt so guilty for intentionally upsetting our sensitive six-month-old puppy. I discontinued the training immediately. I didn't expect to leave Harry outside on his own much in the middle of winter anyway.

In the springtime we repeated the training process. This time Harry was mature enough to learn his perimeter without being frightened by the process. And from then on, he has been very well-trained to the Invisible Fence.

Based on my experience with Harry, I waited until puppy Tory was at least eight months to begin her Invisible Fence training, with refresher guidance from the service company. And all went very smoothly. And of course, she also had Harry as her role model.

To teach the dogs to exit our property with me intentionally, I removed their collars and commanded, "Cross." I left our yard by our front driveway, encouraging them to follow. Of course, there was some hesitancy when the dogs had been recently trained to obey the Invisible Fence boundaries. Eventually, they presumed they were safe to cross if either Jesse or I accompanied them.

The dogs understood staying within their perimeter when we left them in the yard and drove away. But attempting to leave the dogs when we departed other than by car presented a different challenge. Since we already allowed our dogs to run off our property when we were with them, with their IF collars removed, our springers came to expect to accompany us as we left the property on foot.

But then I began riding my bicycle for exercise. If it's a nice enough day for me to cycle, it is also nice enough to leave the springers outside in my absence. To minimize confusion, I chose to leave with my bike by the back driveway. Of course, their collars were on as I repeatedly said, "Stay!"

Fortunately, that worked. I was able to leave by bicycle, and the dogs remained in our yard. I hoped the dogs had learned that they are not permitted to accompany a biking excursion. So, I pushed my luck and attempted to bike from our house by the front driveway, all the while repeatedly commanding, "Stay!" Both Harry and Tory were sitting on our front lawn as I biked away, prematurely congratulating myself on my exit achievement. Within a tenth of mile, I heard Tory charging behind me on the road, with Harry hot on her heels. They had breached the invisible fence while still wearing their electronic collars. I had to dismount my bike and herd them to my side, walking them along the narrow, winding road back to our property, watching out for passing cars. I remembered to remove their collars before the property line so they would not be deterred or shocked on reentering our yard.

Still attempting to bike off-property while leaving the dogs outside on that same pleasant summer morning, I reattached their collars. Repeatedly announcing, "Stay!",

I headed out the back driveway, crossing the Invisible Fence boundaries—and so did the dogs, charging across to join me, ignoring the electronic signal and shock. In the approach-avoidance life lesson, I suppose they learned the reward of joining me was stronger than the fear of the shock.

Once again removing their collars to reenter our boundaries, I had to give up on half of my plan. I left the dogs in the house so I could bike away without their tailing me but also pondered what kind of retraining I might need to ensure their remaining in the yard when I departed by bicycle in the future.

Several weeks later I made a repeat attempt at a clean bike getaway with Harry and Tory in the yard. When I leave the dogs at home, whether in or out, I always give them good-bye dog treats. On that beautiful August morning, I snapped on the dogs' Invisible Fence collars and encouraged them outside with me. In the same way that I would typically leave alone by car, I commanded "Sit!" to them in the driveway. Even though thirteen-year-old Harry rarely maneuvered his arthritic body into the full sit position, I handed over the good-bye biscuits to both dogs that signified my leaving without them. I quickly aimed my bicycle toward the back driveway where most prior getaways had been successful.

"Stay, stay!" I firmly repeated, hoping Tory would not chase me and likely activate Harry to do the same. I avoided looking back. I hoped the Invisible Fence perimeter would resume its originally effective deterrence. No pounding paws pattered behind me as I turned onto the road. Phew! A clean getaway. All future bike departures with dogs outside would be by back driveway to differentiate dog-permissible property outings by front driveway.

I still love the Invisible Fence. I can leave the dogs outside unattended, weather permitting, whether I am in the house or have left the home for a while. The dogs get far more exercise, having the run of the yard rather than being confined inside. And when I come home, they are tuckered out, not driving me crazy for more exercise. It's definitely a win-win situation.

Chapter 5

Legacy to Liza

Biology dictates that the family dog will never outlive the family. We suburban families tend to get pups when our kids are of elementary school age, and they leave us for doggy heaven somewhere around the college years. Canine companionship may be a little-mentioned developmental stage of family life, but it's one whose social and emotional components are comprised of interactions and memories that may last a person's whole life long.

So here's the true tale of our short-tailed dog, so that in the telling I might honor her and she might represent "Every Dog" in any family dog tale ever told.

We got the call from our pet sitter Vinny when we were at an out-of-town family event. It was not totally unexpected. Liza, our darling family dog of almost fifteen years, had been on a long downhill slide of physical incapacitation and doggy dementia for the past year.

There had never been an acute crisis, but little by little our loving English springer spaniel, despite having received a relatively clean senior canine bill of health the prior year, was deteriorating in a multitude of capacities: impaired vision, hearing, walking, sitting, standing, negotiating stairs, and who knew what else on the inside.

Liza had probably embarked on her inevitable journey of aging even earlier than we recognized, but the changes became much more noticeable when we moved to a new family home less than a mile away. The friendly brown and white pooch who used to roam freely and purposefully in our old neighborhood could no longer be let loose. Not only was she likely to return to our old house to take up familiar surveillance on the front lawn, but any calls for her would fall uselessly upon virtually deaf ears.

The streetwise dog who was a neighborhood favorite among both children and adults never seemed to be at ease in our new surroundings. I doubted that she was even making new memories. Each day at our new house seemed to be one of relearning. And to make matters worse, if our aged family pet confusedly walked herself into an inside corner, she could not back herself out. Rather Liza would make some pitiable doggy moan that would send me running to extricate her.

The scenarios were often as comical as they were sad. We knew this diagnosis could be pronounced for a broken car transmission, but who ever heard of a dog that lost its "reverse?"

And eventually her "forward" also seemed to be disintegrating. Finding Liza unable to stand herself up in our absence, our pet sitter took her to the veterinary clinic where she was admitted. Because of her precipitating decline, we family members suspected this would be the final act for our beloved family dog who had for so many years been our high-spirited and entertaining companion, playmate, and devoted friend.

Our timely family get-together presented us with a fitting venue to communally pre-eulogize our longtime pet. We sang forth with fifteen years of Liza stories, starting with the perky puppy that we first met among Lydia's litter of eleven a few weeks post-birth. Bringing her home at seven weeks, we dubbed her "Lydia's Lovely Liza."

Our Liza was filled with good-humored high jinks. Stealing a sneaker, slipper, or stuffed animal, she'd run around the house to elicit a chase. And if by chance there was an open exterior door, she'd run out the portal with her bait and a wily grin that no doubt meant "Come and catch me if you can."

Playful Liza devised her own favorite games and seasonally reenacted them of her own accord. As we unveiled the barbecue grill each spring, Liza would run furiously around the yard to find an errant tennis ball. From her perspective, a backyard deck chef meant a willing throwing arm for her tireless retrieval—not so surprising for a springer spaniel whose pedigree is hailed as a bird dog in the sporting family of canines. Admittedly, Liza was much more into ball sports than bird sports. Not only did she excel at flushing out tennis balls, but she also gamely trapped soccer balls on the lawn and doggy dribbled basketballs in the driveway.

Leaping Liza developed her own winter sport, a combination of a jump shot and keep-away. When our kids went out fully bundled for snow play, Liza sprightly sprung up to snatch the hats off their heads. This was no major crisis for my kids who'd rather go hatless anyway, but Liza's antics eventually precluded her accompanying us to any public sledding area where she deemed any kids' hats fair game.

When Stacy or Ben left home by bike, they urged, "Keep Liza inside," rightly anticipating a determined tailing by their persistent pup. But even after a ten-minute head start, sleuthing Liza would bolt out the door, aim nose to the ground, pick up a scent, and invariably bound off in the biker's direction.

At least Liza's love of bike trailing worked well when she arrived home filthy from mud season meanderings. I'd jump on a bike to lead my mud-caked canine to the nearby brook. "Jump in and clean off," I commanded, and she seemed to know just what I meant.

When roller blades became the rage, Ben thought he'd try "harnessing" Liza for his personal pulley—a very short-lived idea. Someone ended up with a lot of bruises, and it wasn't the dog. Less dangerously, Ben also brought Liza on occasional windsurfing escapades on nearby Nonesuch Pond.

Our faithful dog watched "her" kids board the school bus each morning and raced to the sound of its rumbling return to greet their afternoon arrival. Liza was the constant friend who cuddled close by when either one was sick or lonely. She alternated sleeping accommodations between Stacy and

Ben but kept vigil at the top of the stairs until all family members were home for the night.

As our growing kids became less available daytime companions, the smiley springer befriended young neighborhood children whose repeated pettings and paw shakings were always patiently permitted. Pet-less families kept dog bones just for Liza who made daily rounds to visit kids and collect her treats. My neighborhood identity was primarily "Liza's mom."

This special spaniel's life was one of legends. Toddlers would actually knock at our door to see if Liza could come out to play. A pet sitter who lived nearby would tell Liza, as he let her out of our house in the morning, "Come and see me later." She understood him, he insisted, and she always stopped by on her roving route. When untimely death befell a neighborhood grandfather, Liza stayed steadfastly in the family's yard as callers came and went. The mourning family was convinced that Liza was consoling them, although I secretly credited her behavior to the possibility of tasty food handouts.

Even as Liza aged, she loved being outside in all seasons and temperatures. In summer she dug a cool, shallow nest in the shrubbery beds. In bitter cold she lay on sun-splashed snow until I insistently coaxed her to an indoor vantage point.

After her self-mapped neighborhood rounds, she might sleep so exhaustedly in front of our house that we good-humoredly initiated our "dead checks." Approaching close enough to check for breathing, we ensured that our seemingly paralyzed pet was still among the living. Unfortunately, her dead dog imitation gave more than one concerned pet sitter an unintended scare.

Observing Liza's sometimes arthritically contorted nighttime positioning, Jesse would insist we seek veterinary intervention. But by morning the prior night's immobile invalid miraculously reverted to her sprightly springer self with little evidence of incapacitating infirmity. Go figure.

Toward the end Liza could not keep up with our family joggers. Yet at thirteen-and-a-half years old, she managed to disappear in the power outage of a whopping April Fools' snowstorm and circuitously wend her way back to our old house. In several more months she could no longer keep up with my fast-paced exercise walk but still managed to sneak off our property to disappear into another snowy night the following winter.

By flashlight, foot, and vehicle we searched the dark to no avail. I truly expected to stumble in daylight across a frozen brown and white corpse semi-camouflaged by a landscape of the same two colors. Yet our disoriented dog incredibly survived the night, huddled by a neighbor's brick chimney. Discovering her in the morning, he kindly brought the shivering wanderer inside, warmed her by his fire, and called her dog tag phone number, which was answered by the most grateful pet owner imaginable.

Once fully defrosted, Liza seemed no worse for her adventure and just resumed her life as the same aging fourteen-year-old. Of course, applying the time-worn algebraic equation of seven dog years to one human one, we were talking about a senior citizen in the ninety-plus range.

So when we were pre-eulogizing Liza before her final demise, we all agreed that she had led an incredible dog's life. There was little need to be sad because her dog life was long, happy, and adventure-filled.

Yet with some trepidation I went directly from the airport to the veterinary clinic to make the final decision. I tearfully embraced Liza in a big bear hug as she wobbly stood to greet me in her hospital cage. Unlike some prior veterinary episodes, there was no professional suggestion that our failing pet ought ever to come home. But I declined the offer to watch a supposedly peaceful, sleep-inducing euthanasia. So with some slight ambivalence I left Liza to their merciful procedure and arrangements for disposal.

Passing by the clinic the next day, I thought to inquire whether they had saved Liza's collar and dog tags—a consideration that had not crossed my mind during the prior day's emotional good-bye.

"Sure, I can get it for you," said the receptionist and headed to retrieve my request. "Let me put this in a bag," she said upon returning.

"I don't really need a bag," I told her.

"But it's pretty cold," she explained somewhat sheepishly. Then I caught on. She had just removed the collar from my freezer-stored dog. A chill ran right through me as the assistant held out the small bag.

So, how was I to quell the upsetting feeling of knowing that a lifeless Liza was temporarily frozen solid in advance of removal for cremation? But then I reminded myself, driving teary-eyed toward home, how the cold was no problem for Liza—a dog who loved outings on freezing days and sleeping off her exertions on a snow-packed lawn. Now, I told myself, she was just in a chilled state of eternal asleep. We could both rest easy.

Chapter 6

Doggy Empty Nest

Wonder and exhaustion filled my life again when I brought puppy Harry home. I rightly anticipated the busy work and cuddly rewards but was curiously surprised how friends made immediate dates to visit me and my fetching two-month-old fur ball.

The common theme emerged. Our situation was a living example of replenishing the "nest" first evacuated by grown children pursuing higher education then further emptied by the expiration of the beloved family dog. In the throes of nurturing aging canines or grieving recent dog deaths, my friends were weighing choices—replacement of the family's best friend versus the freedom of "doglessness."

My decision had a slightly different wrinkle. When we said good-bye to Liza, our darling English springer spaniel of nearly fifteen years, we still had her six-year-old "sister" spaniel Chelsea at home. But parenting a mature dog was a snap compared to caretaking an aging canine or raising an energetic puppy.

Indeed, not until we put Liza to sleep did I realize how much of my day was devoted to my geriatric dog: carrying our arthritic animal up and down our several entrance steps; patiently walking, watching, and waiting for our hearing- and vision-diminished pet to relieve herself; extracting our "reverse-less" dog from interior corners into which she entrapped herself; cleaning up after accidents; and administering medications to an ornery patient.

Aging Liza became increasingly irritated by her twice-daily pill regime. Angrily anticipating my longtime method of rapid oral pill insertion and neck rubbing to induce swallow, Liza chomped down faster than I could extricate my fingers. In self-defense, I devised a new pilling process: the peanut-butter hors d'oeuvre, eagerly swallowed with buried pill undetected.

Although Liza's caretaking was admittedly burdensome, I did not rush to put our ailing Alzheimer's-like dog to sleep. But when it was time to say the final good-bye to our devoted family pet, there was one more decision yet to be made: how to dispose of her body.

The veterinary clinic provided a brochure of options ranging from marked burial in a pet cemetery to individual cremation with return of ashes. With our house already filled with pictorial Liza memorabilia, I chose a less expensive option—mass cremation—but also made a monetary donation to the Animal Rescue League in Liza's memory. Of note, I usually make similar contributions to memorialize friends' beloved pets too.

Until I even considered embarking on puppy mothering, I needed a year's recuperation from geriatric dog care. But as soon as I announced little Harry's arrival at our household, two friends arranged to visit right away. Like me, both had lived with wonderful family dogs—the ones you get when your kids are in primary school but who inevitably decline as the grown children are out of the house.

Ivy's sprightly English cocker spaniel Zack had recently died. Jill's handsome black standard poodle Boomer was deteriorating rapidly. Thoughts of replacing the family dog were on both friends' minds.

But the decision can be complex and multifaceted. First, do we really want another dog? Would we prefer the freedom from dog caretaking to the warm presence of a furry friend? Can we handle the demands of puppy raising and training again?

And if the answer to replacement is yes, what kind of dog do we want, regarding breed, gender, and age? A close replica of our first love, or would the same type invite too many unfair comparisons? And what about the preferences of our spouses and our frequently absent but still opinionated grown kids?

A different breed had crossed my mind. I'd been eyeing the shaggy, bear-like Bernese mountain dog for quite some time. But their huge size deterred me. So I stayed faithful to the compact English springer spaniels, the breed with which I'd had sixteen years of familiarity. I chose a male for a change but still selected the brown and white coloring of my prior spaniels. So my dog-loving friends came to meet Harry but also to see a bounding young puppy and his effects on his mature caretaker, me.

"I adore Harry," I told them. "I love watching this cute, furry wanderer energetically explore his world until he flops down exhausted from his overexertions." But at the same time I admitted, "Harry's not the only one flopping down in exhaustion. I'm on my feet constantly, only resting when Harry does."

But I focused on the bright side. In constant motion with hardly a chance to eat, I'd inadvertently discovered a successful weight loss regime: the harried (or, in my case, "Harry-ed") puppy owner's diet and exercise program.

Puppy mothering was also time-consuming: three daily feedings, frequent outings to reinforce house training, and vigilant attention to a surprisingly destructive teether. Harry still managed to destroy a dog bed, decimate my husband's loafers, and gnaw sizeable chunks out of the family room couch and kitchen buffet table.

Leaving Harry caged too long by day made me feel guilty. His plaintive mid-night crying upset my sleep-deprived husband who finally plopped four-month-old Harry in our bed. The coddled canine instantly slept like a baby and forevermore claimed our bed as his.

Before too long "doglessness" did not feel right to either Jill or Ivy. Without her constant companion Boomer, Jill felt lonely. Yet she was experiencing back problems and seriously wondered whether she could manage an active puppy. Connecting with the poodle rescue league solved Jill's dilemma. They found Riggs, a charming, chocolate-colored standard, whose owner had chosen to give up the year-old pooch.

No prototype of Boomer, Riggs came with his own distinct personality and preferences. More manageable than a young pup, Riggs was still playful and adaptable, quickly filling the poodle void in Jill's life. "I can't believe how long he'll keep playing ball with me," observed my friend Jill, who bears a curious resemblance to a poodle by virtue of her distinctive head of tight, thick, wavy brown curls. "Riggs wants to sleep by our bed. Boomer never did that," observed Jill, who admittedly epitomizes the example of an owner who looks like her dog.

Ivy considered switching breeds to minimize comparisons but in the end adopted another adorable black and white male English cocker puppy. Kobi was as winning and intelligent as Zack, but puppy mothering seemed more demanding. And no doubt it was. Ivy's husband urged prompt training to return their house to normalcy, yet no kids were at home to entertain the feisty little guy.

Kobi might need more playtime, Ivy initially worried, than she and her husband were available to give. But as quick-witted Kobi matured through his first year, he permanently endeared himself as Zack's worthy successor. And eventually, Ivy conceded, she developed an even closer bond to Kobi whose devotion was not divided between as many family members.

Like Kobi following Zack, and Riggs succeeding predecessor Boomer, Harry filled the paw prints of our lovely Liza. Yes it was true that we never let Liza sleep in our bed. So maybe we spoiled Harry, rather like indulgent grandparents. But in one special way Harry was trained astoundingly better than all my past dogs.

Every morning Harry heroically retrieved the *Boston Globe* from the bottom of our long downhill driveway and proudly presented his delivery on return to the house. As Harry dutifully exchanged the *Globe* for a dog biscuit, I always said, "Good dog, Harry, great job!" But I suspect he loved the verbal praise even more than his treat.

Chapter 7

Trained to Deliver

Dogs have to be trained, more or less, to socialize them into your lives and protect them from potential harm. Our first dog Lance was wild and crazy. That's actually a trademark of Irish setters, but I had ignorantly selected the breed for the handsome rugged good looks rather than temperament. So for marital and self-preservation, I enrolled Lance in weekly dog training classes in Phoenix. It was well worth the seventy-five-mile round-trip from our home on the Gila River Indian Reservation. We had a serious, no-nonsense instructor who taught commands to be corrected firmly and immediately by choke collar. Even my husband was impressed to see our previously incorrigible setter responding to direct training and learning to consistently obey commands to sit, stay, down, come, and heel. Lance and I even entered some AKC-sanctioned novice training competitions, and he/we did tolerably well.

Our second Irish setter Brandy didn't get the organized class experience, but Lance and I taught her what we already knew. Either Lance was a good role model or Brandy was a lot less headstrong—probably a bit of both.

All my English springer spaniels have had some measure of training, whether organized puppy training and socialization classes and/or my own combination of individualized training. Most of the time we did OK with a moderate amount of rudimentary training. With some tasty treats, they learn fairly quickly the meaning of "come." But admittedly they can be stubborn as to when they will heed the command, especially when chasing after some delectable, doggy-detectable scent on a woodsy walk. Another tough task is preventing easily excitable springers from jumping on arriving people. Fortunately, with age they lose some of their natural spring. At least I have been fairly successful in discouraging my dogs from hopping on my bed when the spread is still in place with the use of some strongly worded "no's" and shoves.

But our third springer Harry became my superstar of canine trainees because of what he learned. When Harry came to live with us in August as a six-week-old puppy, he immediately joined the part of my morning routine that included obtaining *The Boston Globe* from its delivery placement at the bottom of our long downhill driveway. Harry had to go out anyway for his morning business. Then I would head toward the newspaper. Early on Harry took a strong interest in the paper. As I would bend down to pick it up, he would spring ahead to grab it in advance of me.

Fortunately, I saw this as a teachable moment. I could finally put to practical use the behavior theory I had learned as a psychology major at the University of Pennsylvania. Applying Skinnerian principles developed in rat and pigeon training, I rewarded successive approximations of the desired behavior. My goal was to eventually send Harry for the newspaper from inside our house so that I would not even need to step outside my warm abode. Except for summer, the majority of Boston area mornings vary from chilly to frosty to absolutely freezing.

So I began bringing a dog treat with me when Harry and I headed to the newspaper. And as we approached the paper, I would firmly voice the same command: "Newspaper, Harry." And once he picked it up, I would trade him the treat for the paper. Every day I would say, "Newspaper, Harry," from further away from the paper than I had announced the day before. So Harry would run ahead of me to pick up the paper. Eventually, I was standing by the house at the top of the driveway, and Harry would run cheerfully downhill to retrieve the newspaper, returning proudly back to me with paper prey in mouth. Before long I could say, "Newspaper, Harry," from inside the house as I opened the garage, and Harry would go flying out to do his job.

With his return indoors, we always traded newspaper for dog treat. But I am fairly certain that the treat was never Harry's greatest motivation. He instinctively loved to retrieve the newspaper. It was in his genes. And he always seemed to know he had pleased me by doing his daily job.

Indeed, so excited about his job at first, Harry would initially snap up neighbors' newspapers when we walked down our street. That led to a bit of anxious training on my part to deter him from collecting off-property papers.

As our new puppy Harry had come into a home already occupied by our seven-year-old springer Chelsea, I was careful not to foster favoritism or sibling rivalry. So, I always gave Chelsea a treat each time I rewarded Harry's newspaper delivery. Chelsea had never taken any interest in newspaper retrieval, which did not surprise me. Unlike her older "sister" Liza and younger "brother" Harry, Chelsea never even cared to retrieve a tennis ball. Yet Chelsea, who adored any kind of extra food handouts, was just as eager as Harry for the morning delivery job, knowing she would also be a treat recipient upon Harry's completion of his task.

For years, any early morning stirring in the bed by me would lead to a flurry of doggy activity, as both Harry and Chelsea excitedly anticipated my arousal to set in motion the newspaper retrieval process. Once I fully arose, they impatiently attended my morning bathroom routine in eager anticipation of the garage door send-off to newspaper fetching and consequent rewards.

Admittedly, we had a few setbacks. Once Harry became trained to an Invisible Fence®, he was understandably hesitant to pick up the newspaper near the buried "fence" perimeter. So one time when Harry's trustworthy duty to newspaper retrieval coincided with a precariously close paper placement to the fence line, Harry was accidentally zapped by his IF collar. Then I almost lost my newspaper delivery dog. That's not to say I lost the dog. Fence collar zappings are intentionally fully survivable. But the behavior linked to becoming "zap-ably" close to the electronic fence wire is what becomes shunned or eliminated. I had to carefully retrain Harry in opposition to the accidental aversive conditioning he had received. And every so often, I've had to retrain the *Globe* delivery person, by aversive phone calls to superiors, to toss the paper far enough up the driveway, thus further removed from the Invisible Fence line.

Sunday mornings were originally problematic, more so for us than for young Harry. Although the voluminous

Boston Sunday Globe is typically three times as large as the daily, Harry's retrieving instinct was not daunted. If he was not accompanied to assist Sunday paper retrieval, we commonly found sections strewn haphazardly across our lawn, while Harry pranced inside just as proudly with the emptied plastic newspaper cover bag. After a while, a maturing Harry became surprisingly adept at carrying the entire *Sunday Globe* uphill securely in his mouth until disgorging the wide load—at least inside the garage, if not completely up the several interior garage steps to fully enter the house. That was close enough for me.

If Harry was let out of our house very early in the morning, he would try to find the paper before I even sent him or before it had arrived. He would sit observantly in the yard until the driver tossed the newspaper onto our driveway and then swoop downhill to retrieve it. If he had been let outside the house through our sliding glass back door, he conscientiously returned there, patiently clutching the paper in his muzzle.

One morning the phone rang especially early. The *Globe* delivery service called to report that our appropriately delivered newspaper had been dognapped. If we did not find our paper that morning, our paper deliverer wanted us to know where to place the blame—on the dog, not him.

Admittedly, it was impossible to explain to Harry when the occasional paper was inexplicably missing or plowed under by a snowplow. He would return to the house quite dismayed at his inability to fulfill his morning duty.

A Top Dog contest in a 2009 *Chico's* catalog caught my attention. Why a women's apparel company was sponsoring a Top Dog contest was curious to me. But nevertheless

I thought Harry was worthy of the honors. I submitted my written rationale in the required 250 words or less. Here's what I wrote:

> My dog Harry, a nine-year-old English springer spaniel, can't wait for me to get out of bed in the morning so I can let him outside to "retrieve" our *Boston Globe* newspaper from the end of our long downhill driveway and bring it to me inside. I always give him a dog biscuit, but I think his reward is just being able to do his "job" every morning. Starting when he was a puppy, Harry took an interest in the newspaper when he accompanied me as I went out to get it. So step by step, I trained him to pick up the paper and give it to me, allowing him to run ahead of me to get it and bring it back to me as I stayed further away from the paper and provided the command, "Newspaper Harry." Now I just open the door and say the words, and Harry flies down the driveway. As a psychologist, I believe that the best use of my behavioral psychology understanding was training Harry to get the newspaper. He even manages to carry in the entire Sunday edition, although in his younger years sections of the voluminous Sunday paper ended up strewn across our yard.

Shortly thereafter we brought a new puppy home, and I was too busy to remember that I'd even entered the contest. But several months later, I was surprised to receive an e-mail with the subject line "You're a Top Dog Runner-Up!" A senior copywriter from Chico's wrote to me:

> "We loved your Top Dog submission so much, we've chosen you as a runner-up in our Top Dog contest. Congratulations!
>
> As a runner-up, your first name, last initial, dog's name, and hometown will be featured on our website, along with a quote from your story."

Of course, Harry had always been a Top Dog to me. Now countless midlife women shoppers would know that too.

So when we brought the new puppy into our household after Chelsea died of old age, our new springer Tory quickly adapted to the morning routine. Like Chelsea before her, Tory became very excited to cheer on Harry's daily newspaper fetching feat. I doubted that Tory originally understood the whole process, but she was definitely all over the reward at the end of the delivery. So Tory became just as enthusiastic as Chelsea had been to run out of the house with Harry and ultimately receive the treat for the job that Harry did so well.

Three years ago, however, we had a huge shift change in the dynamics of newspaper retrieval at our house. Ten-year-old Harry needed an operation to repair a torn cranial cruciate ligament of his rear left leg. The canine CCL is comparable to the ACL or anterior cruciate ligament of the human knee, as dogs' ligaments are identified by cranial (head) or caudal (tail), while human ligaments are known as anterior (front) or posterior (back). Postoperatively, Harry was absolutely forbidden to run loose for two months. All outings had to be on leash.

Now what was going to happen to my reliable newspaper delivery? Would Harry be upset to be prevented from his job? Would he eventually resume his task when he was finally allowed to run loose again? Would the operation disrupt the best training I had ever developed with any one of my dogs? I had no idea.

With Harry admitted to Tufts University veterinary hospital, Tory woke up alone with me. But she was still eager to maintain the usual morning routine. Ten-month-old Tory ran out of the house, as I announced differentially, "Newspaper, Tory!" I curiously watched out the window as Tory ran toward the paper, but only halfway, seemingly confused as to why Harry wasn't there to grab the *Globe* and bring it inside as usual. So I joined her outside on that frosty November morning, walking toward the paper. We picked the *Globe* up together, and Tory happily carried it back inside, cheerfully anticipating the retrieval treat, which I presented indoors.

I always thought that Harry's newspaper retrieval learning was amazing and personally marveled at my optimal results by implementing successive approximation training. I never imagined I would have any other dog so devoted to this task. But Tory exceeded my expectations. The following morning when we popped out of bed, Tory ran immediately to the garage door. She went flying out of the house to the pronouncement of "Newspaper, Tory." Without any more prompting, Tory tore down the driveway and swiftly returned, *Globe* in mouth, to disgorge the paper and claim her delectable dog biscuit. I quickly realized that the value of vicarious learning cannot be underestimated, even in canines.

In only two days, Tory owned this job. But admittedly I worried how Harry would react to being unceremoniously replaced. However, Harry had no choice upon returning home post-op. He had to be held on leash for every outing for two months. Tory continued to charge out of the house for morning newspaper retrieval, and both dogs received the anticipated return treat. If Harry was upset, he had no way to tell me.

Ever since Tory took over newspaper delivery, she has been even more intent than Harry on fulfilling the task. When I let her out of the house through the garage, she speeds to the exterior garage door faster than I can press the garage door opener. Her front paws rapidly scratch the door before it starts to open, and she squeezes her chunky muscular torso under the door that is not rising fast enough for her eagerness. Tory returns in a flash to deposit the paper with me and claim her edible prize.

Once Harry was allowed to run free again, I wondered if the two of them would be battling over newspaper retrieval. Having not forgotten his many years of *Globe* delivery, Harry appeared enthusiastic to return to his routine. But Tory always got the best of him. She always ran faster and beat him to the paper. He would follow her back inside, seemingly without too much distress, and claim the usual treat. Eventually, Harry didn't even run outside but started waiting with me at the door for Tory's return and consequent treat. "Why bother?" seemed to become his attitude.

But Harry did not give up completely. As our newspaper began arriving much earlier than before, only the two old men of the house, Harry and Jesse, were awake. Initially Tory, like me, had no interest in being out of bed or the house at five a.m. or earlier. So Harry proudly discovered and retrieved the newspaper when Jesse let him out before dawn. However, that left Tory perplexed when I did not send her upon later arousal for the newspaper, which I already noticed to be in the kitchen. But my dear husband, recognizing the importance of this task to both dogs, would sometimes leave the newspaper, originally retrieved by Harry, outside again as he left for work, kindly giving Tory the opportunity to retrieve it as well.

Eventually, Tory caught on that the "early bird catches the worm," or in this case, the early dog fetches the newspaper. She began listening for the early arriving newspaper delivery. And despite her original sleeping-late inclinations, Tory began popping out of bed, however early, to be the primary paper retriever.

Admittedly, I seem to read *The Boston Globe* less and less, with all the news bombarding me through Internet, e-mails, and the multitude of local and cable TV news stations. Additionally, the cost of delivered newspapers has doubled lately. Ordinarily we cancel the newspaper when we are traveling. So recently I tried an experiment while Jesse was traveling but I was still at home. I canceled the *Globe* to see if I would miss it. Without the daily *Globe* awaiting my reading at meals, I appreciatively found time to peruse our community newspaper and a variety of magazines that I had been neglecting. But I had not taken Tory into the experimental equation.

When I arose in the morning, Tory still excitedly ran to the garage door to perform her morning task. But I called her to exit by the sliding glass door to avoid further confusion. Nevertheless, Tory came back inside looking disappointed and befuddled each time there was no newspaper to retrieve. There was no explaining to her about the missing paper and why it had not been delivered. Tory retreated to her kitchen dog bed. Her body language expressed depression, head down between front legs, eyes cast upward to me in a sadly futile way. Admittedly, I may be anthropomorphizing, but I still felt quite guilty about taking away her important job.

E-mailing Jesse in Austria with the subject line "Cancelled Globe," I wrote,

> "Like I said, I canceled while u r away to see if I care
> to have it
> I may not care, but Tory does!
> I forgot to take her into consideration
> May be good reason to keep getting paper :)"

Jesse replied by e-mail, "she lives for that." So we are going to keep getting *The Boston Globe* on a daily basis or possibly switch to *The New York Times.*

Two retrievers are better than none

Chapter 8

Sporty Adventure Dogs

Heading west in our Jeep Commando piled high with camping gear and our portable Klepper kayak, we felt very sporty for a young urban couple. We soon chose sporty Irish setters to accompany our sporty Arizona lifestyle. From our home base on the Gila River Indian Reservation south of Phoenix, we economically traveled, camped, hiked, and boated throughout southwestern United States and Mexico. And the dogs came too. We could travel quite far on any given weekend along Arizona's wide-open highways and bi-ways, especially before lower speed limits were federally imposed due to the oil embargo of the mid-1970s.

Our hiking companions Lance and Brandy ran excitedly by our side as we appreciated the naturally diverse scenery of Arizona: the cactus-laden Sonoran Desert; the red rocks of Sedona and nearby winding Oak Creek Canyon; the pine forests of Flagstaff, Prescott, and Payson; and the rocky ledges and dry brush of the Superstition Mountains.

"What's that ringing sound?" I asked Jesse as we were hiking on the piney White River Apache reservation.

Breaking into a clearing, we found Lance and Brandy had rounded up a frightened herd of bell-collared cows. Who knew our sporting dogs were also herding dogs? The barking setters looked as surprised at their prowess as we were bemused by their inadvertent skill. Doubting the Indian cattle owners would appreciate the humor of this scene, Jesse and I discovered our own herding skills as we quickly rounded up and collared our calamitous canines.

Appropriately leashed on other occasions, we walked straining setters through traditional Native American villages of the Navajo and Hopi. Tethered by our sides, they also visited spectacular national park trails: the rim of the Grand Canyon, the Painted Desert, the Petrified Forest, and Organ Pipe Cactus National Monument. We paraded Lance through Utah's Bryce Canyon among stunning terrain of spiraling rock formations. We held the setters close at Zuni and Acoma pueblos on high mesas of New Mexico.

With their dog food and extra fresh water as cargo, the setters camped with us on the public Mexican beaches at Rocky Point (aka Puerto Peñasco), Guaymas, and Hermosilla. They swam with us in the warm water of the Gulf of California and were ballast as we kayaked the Klepper® out to sea, scanning the waves for playful leaping dolphins.

Kayaking in seas or lakes with our excitable setters was often a challenge, as any intriguing sight was cause for standing and barking, which could ultimately result in toppling out of the kayak. Fortunately, the toppler was usually a dog, not a person. And the kayak did not capsize due to unplanned doggy disembarkation. Lifting a soggy, flailing dog back into the kayak was the greater challenge. Sometimes we tried to leave the dogs onshore to avoid the jumping out and tugging in, but that was rarely a successful strategy.

Lance would keep swimming to reach us no matter how far from shore we paddled, while we worried about his wearing himself out and requiring canine lifesaving skills. Brandy would stay on land but anxiously run along the shoreline, barking incessantly, irritating us and anyone else who happened to be within earshot.

But of course we had to bring our sporty dogs with us when we were on adventures. That's the whole point of owning sporty dogs. We had fun doing sporty activities and watching our dogs have fun too.

Once we moved to Boston, where Jesse became a surgical resident and we both became parents, our camping days were essentially over (Jesse tried to convince me otherwise, but I had no interest in mixing tents and diapers). But we still owned sporty dogs, who still could accompany us on woodsy hikes. We learned about literary history with dogs by our side along the wooded trails ringing Thoreau's famous Walden Pond. We also learned that bodies of water in New England that we would have previously taken for lakes are quaintly called ponds.

With baby Stacy strapped in a backpack attached to Jesse, we sometimes wended our way through local trails and conservation lands, dogs deliriously darting down well-trodden paths. Admittedly, as our parenting and working lives became busier and less sporty, Lance and Brandy just took their own dog-scenting hikes in our suburban town of Wellesley with no leash law. Probably some less-than-appreciative town residents wondered, "Who are those unaccompanied sporty dogs?"

Our first English springer spaniel Liza was more of a sporty ball dog. Because that's what our family was doing during her lifetime. Our springer spaniel jovially joined any family ball player in our yard to trap soccer balls, dribble basketballs, or chase tennis balls. When we brought her with us to watch Stacy playing a Weston High School varsity soccer match, how could Liza know that she was not invited to play? What an embarrassment to teenage Stacy when Liza ran eagerly onto the field to trap and dribble the ball. And the game had to be temporarily stopped for dog interference. Apparently, Liza's "parents" were misbehaving too by not appropriately restraining our exuberant springer.

Liza created her own sporty games too. She often played her version of "catch me if you can" by running around the house with a sneaker, slipper, or favorite stuffed animal. And she particularly liked to fly out an open door with her prize to elicit a longer and more exasperated pursuit. When our kids played in the snow, Liza devised her winter steal-and-run game, joyously leaping to grab a hat and playing chapeau keep-away.

Among the Sporting Group of American Kennel Club designations, English springer spaniels were originally bred to be bird hunting dogs for their ability to flush or "spring" birds out of the brush. But our family was not into that type of sporting or hunting. Nevertheless, if Liza observed some wild suburban animal like a squirrel or chipmunk from her interior vantage point, she would bark incessantly until sprung out of the house and then chase maniacally after the feral intruder. Exhibiting the same bravado when a large wild turkey surprisingly strolled through our yard, Liza barked fiercely inside and flew out of an offered door. Unlike the little woodland creatures who always fled the harassing hound, the large feathered beast held her ground. Flustered and confused, Liza did not pursue and cowardly retreated to the house. And that's how our courageous canine earned her family nickname "The Great Hunter."

But maybe it was better to be known facetiously as the Great Hunter than have Harry's hunting debacle when he traumatically tangled with a wild turkey hen protecting her turkey chicks. Running with Jesse on a Martha's Vineyard trail, young Harry chased the chicks, and their mother swiftly retaliated. Due to a pecking wound, Harry developed a severe systemic infection necessitating full-spectrum antibiotic treatment. Faced with an unflinching turkey, I prefer the Great Hunter Liza's strategy: better to retreat to hunt another day.

Just like Liza, our successive three springers have all boisterously barked at the passing creatures that invade our yard. Every mundane squirrel is just as exciting as the one before. Personally, I am much more enthralled to see elegant white-tailed deer meandering through our property than the common sightings of squirrels and chipmunks. But from our springers' perspective, there's no differentiating the bark that announces a flitting flock of birds or a nut-gnashing chipmunk from a stunning stag. And the spaniels bark unrelentingly until let outside to chase the invading aliens up trees, into ground holes, or beyond our boundary. Some savvy local deer, having learned that our sporting dogs will not proceed past certain invisible barriers, will stand boldly beyond our border taunting our emboldened barkers.

Before I release the clamorous canines from our house, I usually try to see what has aroused my springer sentries. Robins and squirrels easily flee to treetop refuge when startled by a charging barrage. Our springers are exercised with little harm to the common visitors. The dogs rarely catch a creature that has found its way into our domain, unless the unfortunate capture is young, ill, or slow.

But I am especially interested to view the less frequent fauna before they are frightened away by the noise and the chase. Despite the occasional deer-munching damage to our plants and shrubbery, I am always delighted to see the majestic ungulates prancing lightly and glancing guardedly on our property. Holding the eager canines inside in hopes that skittish deer will linger longer, I often try to photograph those that are visibly close.

Similarly intrigued to see the lovely variety of birds that visit our personal property, I keep the delirious dogs contained while I enjoy the spectacle of colorful blue jays, scarlet red cardinals, or a rare orange oriole. Redheaded woodpeckers are often heard first before seen. One particularly lovelorn pecker found that he could hammer out his mating call much louder on our aluminum chimney cap than on a tree. As the metallic hammering continued for days, Chelsea's barking similarly escalated but unfortunately had no obvious effect on scaring the pecker from his raucously reverberating perch. I have no way of knowing if the woodpecker was any more successful at obtaining a mate, but I think he may have needed the avian equivalent of a maxillofacial surgeon at the end of his metal-pounding love quest.

The nocturnal hooting of an unseen owl also spurred somnambulant Chelsea into barking spasms, both inside and outside the house. Yet, the hooting continued, the owl unperturbed by our restless canine. Our sleep, however, was greatly perturbed.

Another true bird story: Driving up my driveway on a bright, sunny November day, I shockingly spied an enormous great blue heron unguardedly preening himself at my front door step. Framed under our columned portico, he appeared to be proudly posing for a portrait. Although I had recently seen a great blue heron from afar, walking gingerly on nearby frozen Nonesuch Pond, I would never have imagined this neighborly visit, so up close and personal. Stopping the car, I quietly watched the magnificent bird who grandiosely stood almost four feet tall, with characteristic slate blue plumage, snake-like neck, and elongated beak. I chided myself about having no camera with me. But I did use my cell phone, which unfortunately did not have a built-in camera, to successively call my daughter and mother to excitedly announce the spectacle at my front door. Maybe I can photograph him through windows in my house, I thought. So I slowly drove the car up the driveway to the garage. Amazingly, the bird did not flee at the car's movement or the sound of the opening garage. And surprisingly my bird dogs, who might bark at the sighting of mundane crows or robins, had not noticed the huge heron from their kitchen vantage point. Nor had the heron rung the doorbell, always a dead giveaway to otherwise clueless spaniels. To ensure the dogs' further oblivion and prevent barking bombardment, I quickly gated the dogs in the family room at the back of our house. Grabbing my camera, I tiptoed to the windows aside the front door and carefully knelt down to aim the camera. Just as I was about to shoot, Mr. Heron spread his ample wingspan and soared off, pterodactyl-like, away from our house. No photo evidence, but I still maintain a vivid memory of this magnificent water bird.

Increasingly sighted in our locale, the red-tailed hawk is a stately avian spectacle. But I have admittedly been wary of hawks' potential aggression, especially when our springers were young. In fact, a young boy in our town was leash walking his dachshund near his house when a hawk swooped down and latched his talons onto the unsuspecting pup. Hearing the boy's screams, his father ran from the house and batted the hawk away. Fortunately the little dog's wounds were successfully treated. But the growing hawk population in our area, although handsome to behold, is becoming almost as dangerous to our small pets as roving coyotes.

Yes, coyotes, we have them too, in the wild west suburbs of Boston. I usually presume that the canine cacophony of two excited springers will scare off a lone coyote, and that our full-grown, fifty-pound spaniels are too big to be attacked. But we once had two persistent coyotes hovering at the edge of our backyard when our resident pets were spaniel Chelsea and our cat. Pet sitter Vinny is no fan of coyotes, having sickeningly seen one catch and disembowel his own beloved cat. So, he brought us his trusty BB gun to scare off the lean, mean coyotes. Fortunately for all of us, the wily coyotes eventually left our area before any violence ensued.

Even wilder? What is high in that spruce tree? I asked myself one March day while relaxing in my outdoor spa after playing tennis. Is it a big crow? No, it looks furry but much bigger and blacker than a squirrel. Some other kind of rodent? But what climbs trees? A small bear? No, it has a long tail. Maybe a large coon cat? Exiting the spa and wrapping on my terry bathrobe, I walked closer to eye the unidentified creature. By process of eliminating animals it was not, I guessed and looked up fisher on Wikipedia. I had read in the *Boston Globe* that fishers were becoming increasingly observed in our neck of the woods. Vinny had previously seen this omnivorous predator on his property at the opposite end of our town. That was my first sighting of this forest-dwelling mammal of the weasel family.

Of course, once the dogs got wind of the fisher, their noses guided them to his preferred perch. The fisher remained highly ensconced in the treetop as long as Harry and Tory bellicosely barked below. I much preferred their loud indoor barking to soundly spook the fisher from the tree and out of our yard before the dogs even went outside. I was wary of a potential face-to-face scuffle between our curious canines and this sharp-toothed predator. The fisher, presumably the same one, returned to the same favorite fir tree in March of successive years. From indoors, the dogs often smelled him before I visually noticed the dark, long-tailed creature. Fortunately, no fur ever flew between the furry proprietors and the uninvited visitor.

Woodland animal visitation to our yard is amplified during mating season. Boisterous bucks and pounding woodpeckers are cause for barking alarms but escape unscathed by our fenced and grounded spaniels. But low-to-ground, slow moving reptiles that appear in spring and summer may be in harm's way. A six-inch box turtle, having ventured from his naturally hidden surroundings in search of love, looks and smells a lot like a novel play toy to a youthful sporty spaniel. Hiding head in shell is potentially protective but does not deter a dog from snatching up the entire turtle. I have had to rescue the occasional misguided tortoise from the moist muzzle of a spirited spaniel.

When I was frequently outside accompanying puppy Tory and ailing Harry, I discovered that lots of little frogs and toads populate our property. I simultaneously discovered that puppy Tory liked to pop them in her mouth like little chew toys and was resistant to spit them out. For reasons that are fairly obvious, I was reluctant to insert my hand in her mouth to disgorge a toad. If I first saw the little hopper on the ground, I tried to nudge him elsewhere and distract Tory from noticing an unfortunately attractive living toy.

But I rapidly take a lot more evasive action if I spy a snake in the grass. That sends me into immediate round-up-the-dogs mode, moving them inside ASAP. I do not want to see one of my sporty dogs carrying a wriggling snake in his snout or being bitten by a poisonous serpent. Probably most viper visitors are harmless garden snakes, but I do not want to test that theory. After sequestering the dogs, I curiously return with my camera to obtain photographic evidence before the serpent slithers away.

There are many sports and adventures off-property too, as our sporty spaniels adore accompanying us on exercise endeavors on local roads, trails, fields, and ponds.

Without any announcement by me, the springers intuitively know when I dress for a walking adventure. I have to ban the enthusiastic pups from my bedroom or usher them out of the house to ready myself without being overanxiously accosted. It's not simply donning sporty shoes that excites the dogs, as comparatively no arousal is instantly elicited when I dress in tennis apparel. They seem to have learned the nuances of my attire and behavior that wordlessly says to them, "I am going out to exercise, and you are coming too!"

And after a snowstorm, the exercise may be joining me while I snowshoe in the woods directly from our house. Getting ready can be the most difficult part, as the dogs excitedly bark at my feet in anticipation as I hurriedly adjust the snowshoe buckles with rapidly chilling fingers.

Admittedly, the springers have many and more varied exercise jaunts with Jesse, a runner and cross-country skier, who has traversed most of the surprisingly many woodland trails that our small suburban town has to offer. As some of our town trails are also equestrian, young Harry learned about horses the hard way. Barking up close and personal at a large, unfamiliar mammal earned Harry a swift and memorable kick. Since his one-time life lesson, Harry always gives horses a wide berth. We wish the dogs would also steer clear of fresh horse manure, whose pungent odor is as attractive to canines as it is offensive to humans.

Keeping the dogs relatively clean on sporty hikes presents its own challenges. Marshes, bogs, and fetid lowlands are ubiquitous. We either have to divert the dashing dogs from splashing through swamps of black biodegrading goo or subsequently find clean running water for them to immerse and rinse relatively clean. The mud problem, to my liking, is seasonally solved during winter adventures. The dogs return generally unsoiled, having exercised across snow-covered ground and iced-over wetlands and waterways.

However, winter adventures presented other challenges. We would be out with the dogs, all enjoying the beauty of freshly fallen snow, and come to realize one spaniel was lagging. Where was Chelsea? We looked back and she was intently collapsed on the snow, although she had been springing delightedly only moments before. With the extended outing, the fresh snow had clumped on the feathered long hairs of Chelsea's legs. She was vigorously trying to bite off the uncomfortably cemented snowballs. Her futile attempts only served to exacerbate the problem, as wetted clumps spawned more and larger snowballs. Typically no amount of tugging would release the clinging clumps while still outside in freezing temperatures. But we couldn't explain that to Chelsea or any of our longhaired canines who have been subjected to this wintry predicament. Fortunately, the problem, while temporarily uncomfortable, is not permanent and eventually resolves by indoor melting.

Just like any other sporty outings, our spaniels love to accompany Jesse on his cross-country skiing adventures. While Jesse creates first tracks on newly fallen snow, our spaniels will spring spryly ahead over deep snow and drifts. Their energy is boundless—that is, until their spring has sprung in the late stage of spaniel life. Senior Harry, as Chelsea before him, now patiently paces behind Jesse's snow-flattening tracks, less willing to overly exert and exhaust himself by pouncing his own snow trail.

Sometimes we cross-country ski right across frozen and snow-covered Nonesuch Pond. But when our nearby pond is securely frozen with no soft snow coverlet, it's time to don our ice skates. No skates for the spaniels, but they will not be left on shore, preferring to amusingly slip and slide across the ice as Jesse and I glide on stainless blades, occasionally knocking a hockey puck between us.

Dog sports on ice

Jesse is typically eager to test the surface of newly solidified pond water, but

I am more hesitant to skate until securely certain of sufficient black ice thickness. Every Boston area winter we see television news reports of dogs breaking through thin ice of insufficiently frozen ponds, frantic owners, and heroic rescue efforts. On one especially bitter cold weekend morning, Jesse headed out to exercise with the dogs. At the end of our woodsy lane, we often go to a pond-side day camp property accessed by a small wooden bridge across a stream running into Nonesuch Pond. Where the running stream empties into the pond, the ice forms more slowly and tends to be much thinner than the rest of the seemingly solidly frozen pond.

"I'm a hero!" Jesse proudly announced to me as the icy shivering, dripping wet threesome gratefully returned indoors. "Chelsea crashed through the ice, and I had to go in to save her," Jesse related. "When I was getting Chelsea out, Liza came over to us, and she crashed through too. Then I had to get her out."

"But where were all of you when you crashed through the ice?" I asked accusatorially. "Were you near where the stream empties into the pond?"

"Yes, right by there," Jesse answered, still impressed by his self-nominated heroism.

"You're not a hero!" I exclaimed. "You caused the catastrophe. You wouldn't have had to rescue anyone if you hadn't run the dogs so close to the running water where the ice is so thin." Apparently, the dogs were not our only family members who needed to learn the hard way. But fortunately all was well that ended well, and all three of them defrosted with no permanent cryogenic harm.

Chapter 9

Tennis Ball Tenacity

It's all about the ball!

The most popular sport of our current two springer spaniels is tennis, or rather retrieving tossed tennis balls. Admittedly, Liza enjoyed that too, but she would indiscriminately play with any type of ball, depending which sport the kids happened to be tossing, dribbling, or kicking. When Harry was young, he initially appeared to be developing his bird dog genes, playfully chasing teasing flocks of swallows around the neighboring athletic field. The game appeared to be just as much fun for the birds as Harry. As long as Harry was chasing them, the swallows kept flying in circles over the field, swooping low to the ground, just beyond the reach of a barking, chasing dog, when they could just as easily have flown high and away.

But when Harry learned the human-created game of chasing a fuzzy yellow ball and tirelessly retrieving it for repeated ball tosses, he sadly lost his innate bird chasing interest. However, Jesse found tennis ball tossing to be an ideal way to optimally exercise our highly energetic young spaniel. And fortunately, my being an avid tennis player has generated an endless supply of used tennis balls for canine playtime.

The ideal way, we discovered, to play doggy tennis is with a plastic, long-armed ball thrower, commonly sold in pet stores and packaged with two balls, which tend to be lost immediately. But the thrower has multiple advantages. We can send the balls much farther than by arm toss, which gives the dogs more retrieving exercise. And then they take longer to return with the ball. Particularly for me, not having Jesse's baseball playing talent, my throwing arm is less likely to get sore and worn out. And, as I can scoop up the tennis ball with the cup end to reinsert, I never have to touch the increasingly dirty and slobbery sphere that is repeatedly dropped at my feet with unceasing enthusiasm.

Jesse rarely goes out to exercise himself and the dogs without the ball thrower. Admittedly that has a positive side. Harry stays focused on ball retrieval, too busy to impolitely bark and jump at walkers or runners whose paths are crossed. Yet I am dismayed that Harry, being so ball fixated, misses the full spectrum of surrounding scents that a superb canine olfactory organ can otherwise detect. So I sometimes intentionally walk Harry *sans* ball thrower, refusing his pleas to toss an errant tennis ball that he has discovered along our way. Tossing tennis balls over snow-covered ground is especially futile, as the tossed ball often sinks undetectably below snow surface.

Chelsea never took an interest in ball retrieval. So when Chelsea and Harry were our springer duo, there was never any competition for Harry in the realm of ball chasing. And then along came Tory! Harry was a mature nine year-old springer spaniel when we brought Tory home, but he was never obviously jealous of the new pup sharing his humans' attention. Harry was not originally an only dog, having lived as the younger "brother" to Chelsea for seven years. And from my admittedly anthropomorphic perspective, I thought Harry was relieved to have canine company again after two years of solitary dog life at our house.

Puppy Tory observed right away that her older "brother" Harry loved to retrieve tennis balls, and she decided to join the game on her terms. Initially, her favorite tactic was to steal a ball tossed to Harry and play keep-away. And she was fast. Her strategy was particularly perplexing to Harry, as he always wanted to continue any initiated ball toss event with the same starting ball. There might be a dozen balls littering our yard, but Harry was always determined to locate the specific ball that he had been chasing during any one ball play episode. He seemed to be genetically hardwired for that behavior.

Once Tory caught on to the knack of ball retrieval by returning it to the thrower for repeated tosses, we attempted to use two balls for two dogs. But while Harry always wanted to retrieve the exact same ball with which he started, Tory was indiscriminate about which ball she chased. Much to Harry's chagrin, speedy Tory often beat him to his preferred orb. Eventually, single-minded Harry had to give up the notion that only one ball was retrievably acceptable, and he will now reluctantly chase alternative balls during any given outing.

So when I exercise the dogs off-property with the ball thrower, I start by tossing two balls, initially attempting to differentiate balls and their retrievers. Being ball-fixated, Harry intently tries to keep track of his ball on our walk. Although starting with her own ball, Tory indiscriminately steals Harry's ball and typically drops and loses one or both balls as she distractedly follows exciting woodland scents or jumps in the stream to cool off.

Ever since Tory joined Harry's tennis game, we require a much greater supply of used tennis balls than ordinarily accumulate from my on-court tennis games. I gladly accept additional used tennis balls from tennis-playing friends, and we occasionally scoop extras from the tennis ball recycling bin at our tennis club.

When Vinny pet sits, he does not take the dogs off-property, although he predominantly exercises Harry and Tory with their favorite game of ball retrieval. When Vinny is in charge, the dogs expect the game every time he returns to the house. But, aware that they will not be heading off-property, the dogs will not chase an errant ball that bounces beyond the potentially shocking invisible fence boundary. Our woodsy perimeter is likely identifiable by a boundary of dirty yellow spheres.

From the onset of springer tennis ball interest, I have been emphatically clear to both human and spaniel inhabitants that tennis ball play is an outdoor sport. Crashing canines and bouncing balls are devastatingly damaging to interior domain. Yet, countless tennis balls litter the floor of our house, in corners, under furniture, and under foot, ready for accessible discovery at the least speculation that some person may toss tennis balls outside. At least I try to immediately banish the muddiest and slimiest balls that are playfully carried inside by proud pooches.

Inclement weather does not deter our obsessed spaniels from their indomitable interest in tennis ball retrieving. A recent winter was much colder and snowier than usual, even in our New England climate known for its cold, snowy winters. From December through February, chilling storms deposited rapidly accumulating amounts of snow with little warming and melting between significant frozen events. So how snowy was it? Although plowed and sanded often, our long uphill driveway became so narrowed by steep snow walls that the oil truck could not negotiate delivery, necessitating additional snow excavation by front-end loader. A warming March month was more welcome than usual. As melting snow depth finally exposed bare ground, we most appreciatively viewed the harbingers of spring—newly sprouting shoots of day lilies, hostas, crocuses, and daffodils. But something else was sprouting that year too. The dissipating snow layers uncovered a whole new crop of yellow smiley-faced spheres, joyfully popping out of the warming earth. With their harvest, we were well-supplied with tennis balls throughout the spring.

I am fairly certain that any excavations on our property in the far distant future will unearth an inordinate amount of decaying tennis balls, likely leading to curious speculation about voluminous tennis activity on an undulating knoll.

Chapter 10

Chow Time

From dog one, Lance, through dog six, Tory, the main staple of our dogs' diet has been dry dog food, purchased in large, sturdy, long-lasting bags. The brand and type of dog food has varied over the years, reflective of our income level, age of our dogs, and vet and pet store recommendations.

But we always supplemented their repetitious dry dog food diet with table scraps, leftovers, and many dog treats doled out for exhibited or anticipated good behavior. When we used to eat much more beef in our people diet, the dogs of our younger adulthood were the happy beneficiaries of many mouth-watering steak bones and restaurant doggie bags.

Jesse never left a western steak fry party empty-handed, collecting lots more than just our personal leftovers into as many bags as he could load up. I am not sure who was more excited, my husband or the Irish setters, when Jesse would present Lance and Brandy with a bounty of bones. Jesse was as food crazed for the dogs as a candy-collecting kid on Halloween.

"Don't give them all the bones at once," I would admonish. One or two steak bones per dog might be delightful, but several could be digestively disastrous. Jesse finally got the hint when he was left to clean up the resulting gastric disasters.

Admittedly, our dogs sometimes try to supplement their own diets, especially if people food is temptingly within their reach. I've had a long history of leaving foods far from counter top edges to avoid delectables swiftly swiped into straining front paws. Others have been less suspecting of sneaky dog maneuvers. Chelsea stole a pound of raw hamburger meat from the kitchen counter when Ben was preoccupied with lasagna preparation. And Vinny has disturbingly lost his brown-bagged lunch on several occasions.

The king of food foraging and counter cruising, however, belonged to our relatives, the Kaplans. They could not even use their trash compactor because their table-high Rhodesian ridgeback Rocky learned to open it and scavenge its contents. While humans were socializing nearby, I watched Rocky take a premeditated offensive leap to grab a bagel from the center of their island kitchen counter. The only way to ensure the safety of my home-baked cheesecake from calculating canine consumption was by temporary sanctuary in their microwave oven.

Coffee tables are a bigger problem at our house when cocktails and hors d'oeuvres are being served. Even food stationed in the center of the table is at risk. So we have to remain doggy vigilant when entertaining at snout level. Of course, constant watchfulness is not always possible, especially at house parties. On one New Year's Day brunch, Liza turned my homemade chopped liver into her personal bowl of dog chow. Although chopped liver might seem like dog food to some people, it is actually a human delicacy in our house.

Liza was a wonderful family dog, but she still had her imperfections. Because she knew where her dog biscuits were kept, she would paw the pantry door to make her request known. As the painted wooden door became increasingly scratched, I worried it would become irreparably gouged. I had seen the ruinous results on my friend's pantry door by Airedale Casey's eager meal anticipation. So when Liza scratched the door, I intentionally avoided rewarding her desire. But I carefully watched her kitchen behavior, attempting to award a treat for anticipatory standing or sitting by the pantry before the door was pawed. The undesirable behavior was ignored or circumvented while the preferred behavior was rewarded. Eventually Liza learned to wait patiently by the door for her desired doggy treat—another example of using behavior theory I learned as a psych major to practical good use in dog training.

For years our dogs have been the prewash to our dishwasher. Food remains are enthusiastically licked from plates and pans before disinfecting in scalding hot water and dishwasher soap. A dinner guest was once appalled to learn of this potentially germ-spreading habit, although I tried to assure her that kitchenware that is hand-washed, like wooden cutting boards, do not participate in pooches' palatable prewash.

While our dogs have always been offered table scraps or leftovers, I have prohibited handouts directly from the dining table to prevent bothersome begging behavior. Extremely anxious to lick the leftovers, however, Chelsea decided how long a human mealtime was supposed to last. In her estimation, it was about fifteen minutes. That's how long Chelsea gave us to eat our dinner in peace. Then she would impatiently circle the table, vocally huffing at our lingering meal that delayed her daily leftover fest.

All our dogs liked treats and leftovers, but Chelsea was the most food-obsessed. When Chelsea joined our family as second springer to Liza, there were angry squabbles over leftovers and occasional teeth-gnashing skirmishes under the kitchen table. I never knew which dog to blame, as it was impossible to determine who made the first jealous move. When Chelsea later became top dog and Harry her junior, skirmishes over potential tasty handouts continued to erupt. I suspected Chelsea was the initiating culprit but could not fully condemn her. Maybe she had just learned bad habits from Liza. Or maybe this would happen when any two spaniels anticipated treats. I finally tagged the troublemaker when Tory joined Harry as our two family springers. Like Lance and Brandy many decades gone by, our current pets can politely lick the same plate without any jealous altercation. Fortunately, Harry did not learn bad habits from his older "sister", allowing me to identify Chelsea as the food-fixated aggressor among our spaniels.

While delicious leftovers elicited eruptions, mundane dry dog food could sit out all day and night without any of our first five dogs finishing a full meal. So essentially that's how I fed them: by leaving a perpetually full bowl of dry dog food accessible for consumption by any dog who randomly experienced a hunger pang. From these dogs' perspective, dry kibble was what they ate when there were no better prospects.

When we moved to our current house, aging Liza was stiffly bowing her head to eat or drink from dog bowls on the floor. Noticing a catalog advertisement for a pair of bowls sunken into a raised table, I ordered Our Pets™ Big Dog Feeder, a much more ergonomically preferable feeding arrangement for arthritic Liza.

Chelsea and Harry also ate and drank from Liza's dog bowl table, which has remained next to the door that exits into our garage. When I am leaving the house and the weather is optimal, I prefer to send our Invisibly Fenced dogs outside so they can discover more interesting doggy activities and potentially get more exercise. Apparently recognizing when I would be leaving him outside, Harry developed an anticipatory exit habit. He would pause by the dog food bowl to quickly gobble up a couple mouthfuls of available kibble that he had otherwise taken little interest in that day. Harry seemed to prophylactically tank up to forestall potential hunger pangs when about to be left outside for an indeterminate length of time.

Unfortunately, I can no longer leave dry food in the bowl for random grazing by Harry who is a lean, reluctant eater. That's because chunky Tory is just the opposite—an eager and ravenous feeder who downs her twice-daily allotment of mealtime kibble immediately and with gusto. Surely, she would more than double her food consumption and her weight if allowed to eat at will.

So both Tory and Harry are restricted to measured food bowls at breakfast and dinner, the amount recommended on the package according to dog weight. But we have settled into a curious feeding routine. I always fence Harry into his own temporary eating area to ensure he has time and opportunity to consume his food without interruption. Once I have noticed Harry has quit eating his meal, I release the gate and notice what is left in the bowl. Of course, Tory, who has rapidly chowed down her own meal, runs over to also check out Harry's leftovers. Much more often than not, Harry has not finished his food. So I sit on the nearby stairs, holding and petting Tory.

Lately I am sitting longer and more frequently, impatiently awaiting Harry's interest in his mundane meal. If I walk away, so will Harry. I typically dislike killing time, but this temporary time-out affords Tory my full attention and grants me a few minutes of unintentional but likely beneficial relaxation. Harry often returns to take a few more mouthfuls, as if he wants to please me by continuing to eat. When he finally leaves the bowl, Tory and I both look interestedly to see what's left. If there's a lot, I pick up the bowl to save for the next meal. But if there's just a little left, I let Tory finish up the kibble. And she's developed her own funny habit from often being restrained from eating Harry's food. When allowed access to Harry's bowl, Tory will huff inquiringly in front of the food, as if asking, "Can I eat this now?" And then I have to assure her that she is permitted to finish the food.

To encourage Harry to eat more food, I mix in a few large spoonfuls of moist canned dog food in his dinner bowl. The food is more appetizing to Harry, and he does seem to eat more. A diet of solely canned food is not recommended by our vet or by me. According to Dr. Kyrka, eating mostly dry dog food is optimal for Harry's dental hygiene. While canned dog food is very appetizing to our dogs, its looks and smell are quite distasteful to me. So I only add canned dog food at Harry's dinner meal. I cannot stomach spooning out the wet dog food first thing in the morning. But lately I have been adding a bit of non-offensive chicken broth to Harry's morning meal.

Of course, Tory does not get added canned food or soup because she needs no extra encouragement to eat her dry food. But in the interest of treating Tory fairly, I let her lick the spoon that I use to scoop the wet food into Harry's dinner. And if I distractedly forget, Tory does not. She always reminds me by hanging out expectantly by the kitchen counter until I notice her tasty spoon has not yet been offered.

My encouraging supplements to Harry's diet are minimal compared to our brother-in-law Alan's food preparation for Sammy, his third Rhodesian ridgeback. At only a year old, Sammy had some surprising problems of undetermined origin. Bloated and obese, Sammy was very thirsty, and her hair was falling out. Based on recommendations of Chinese, holistic, and alternative medicine, Alan hand prepared her meals. He slow cooked a combination of one-third beef, one-third brown rice, and one-third vegetable mixture of sweet potatoes, carrots, celery, kale, and broccoli. Fairly soon, Sammy's problematic symptoms disappeared. But devoted dog daddy Alan kept cooking for his dear dog for several years anyway.

Chapter 11

Yucky and Stinky

Disclaimer: If you are squeamish about yucky stuff, you might want to skip this chapter.

A big problem of dog ownership is how dogs are attracted to yucky stuff, getting into situations that are totally disgusting from a human perspective. There's a wide differential between what sends dogs into olfactory ecstasy and what humans find offensively malodorous.

When we began raising our first dog near a small Indian Health Service hospital in Arizona, our Irish setter Lance excitedly discovered that he could occasionally recover a particularly canine-tantalizing treat from the outside trash bins: soiled diapers—totally gross and disgusting. Extracting the pungent possession pilfered by our proud pooch was a task I readily assigned to my physician husband. In his dealings with sick people, Jesse was certainly more accustomed to off-putting smells than me.

Unfortunate for us humans, canines are magnetically drawn to the cologne of biologic decomposition. We learned that early on when Lance returned from exploring the Sonoran Desert with a rotting rabbit. Even after Jesse managed to pry the putrid carcass from Lance's mouth, I was left with the task of disinfecting our stinky setter.

When we brought our second setter puppy into our family, we had another distressing episode due to the vast smell attraction discrepancy between dogs and humans. Because mice had been entering buildings of the Indian hospital compound, rodent poison was placed in our garage. But that's not what Brandy ate. Recognizing d-Con® might be as tasteful to dogs as rodents, the poison was placed on a high shelf. Quite distressingly, however, we discovered six-month-old Brandy excitedly holding a dead mouse in her mouth. When we tried to disgorge her prized prey, she swallowed the whole mouse. The small rodent had likely died from the poisoning ingredient warfarin, a blood anticoagulant, and we had no idea how toxic warfarin inside the mouse would be to our young pup. The vet did not anticipate the worst but recommended administering ipecac to induce vomiting. Several worrisome doses later, Brandy finally regurgitated the mouse. She completely survived the ordeal, which was probably much more traumatic for her human parents than for our puppy.

Moving from the Arizona desert to the woodsy Boston suburbs opened up a wondrous world of potentially yucky escapades. Preventively, we immediately installed an expensive wooden fence at our small Wellesley starter home. But there was no mandatory town leash law at that time, and we abutted a large tract of wooded conservation land. So we occasionally let our highly energetic Irish setters roam free, as much for their sanity as ours. Unfortunately, the woods were not always as attractive as the nearby commercial area where tasty discoveries might be located in garbage bins behind grocery stores and restaurants.

Even much more unfortunately, Lance eventually tangled with the premier creature of powerful and prolonged offensive odor—the otherwise cute critter with the distinctive white stripe on his black body fur. Getting skunked may have been a blow to Lance's pride, but it was shock to our human olfactory sensitivity. Following the 1970s wisdom for skunk scent removal, Jesse washed Lance in tomato juice, dousing our gangly, longhaired, seventy-five-pound reluctant bather in our basement laundry room utility sink. I was left with washing off the red-splattered sink, appliances, and walls. This recommended solution was not a complete fix, as Lance still bore some residual odor of skunky tomato juice, which we had to endure for several more weeks.

By the time we acquired our first English springer spaniel in 1983, we had moved to neighboring Weston, another town with no leash law. Through what I suppose was benign neglect, Liza eventually became an independent, street-wise, neighborhood dog. That worked for me during my busiest, working-mother life stage, as Liza exercised herself without my personal involvement. Upon hearing the familiar paw knock at our raised ranch front door, I was always glad to welcome wandering Liza home—that is, except when she returned too filthy for house entry. During New England spring mud season, Liza might return coated with smelly black goop, having traversed some swampy wetlands on her daily meanderings.

My preferred cleaning tactic was to hop on a bicycle and yell, "Liza, follow me!"

And she always cooperatively ran along with me, an easy quarter mile to the rippling brook at the end of our street. "Go clean off in the water," I would tell her. And Liza would obediently jump in to rinse herself, seemingly understanding exactly what I had in mind. I've often wished Liza could have gone to the brook and clean up on her own without my leading the way by bicycle. But on the other paw, we would have missed all that quality time together.

When we moved to our second Weston home, springer number two Chelsea was initially unrestrained. Without an invisible fence installation, Chelsea eventually recognized she could stray from our house. And fortunately, she also found her way home. But Chelsea's off-property explorations were not without repercussions. She was not being shocked, but sometimes I was when I saw the return of a very filthy Chelsea. Attracted to the nearby swampy area, Chelsea might return covered in black boggy gook. Appearing to recognize an imminent hosing, she would cagily avoid my attempts to catch her. But in the approach-avoidance conflict of food versus bathing, Chelsea could not resist an especially tasty offering. Our mud-caked canine could finally be tempted close enough to leash her by an outstretched hotdog.

So for most of our dog-raising lives, we have continued to find our sporty canines attracted to what we humans consider yucky or even worse. On woodsy hikes, we are particularly disgusted to come upon our front-running dogs chowing down on a fetid mound of horse manure. Or walking lakeside, we might discover our dogs delighting in a bounty of green sausage-like hors d'oeuvres deposited by frequent flocks of Canada geese.

And there was no predicting when a dog might find an especially seductive decomposing deer deposit, which would send her into wallowing ecstasy. Chelsea was the queen of deer doo-doo discovery. She would first rub her nose in the putrid perfume, deeply inhaling the "scent-sational" odor. Finding the odiferous prize extra tantalizing, she would swipe her entire head, ear-to-ear, upon the stinky bounty, allowing total permeation of the odious scent into every cranial orifice. And the final glory was the full corporeal torso rub to ensure long-lasting delight of the rapturous inhalation, but obviously not for me as the one who was going to spend the next hour scrubbing off the malodorous detritus before the stench offensively invaded our carpets, dog-permitted couches, and family bedding.

Since we prefer to walk our dogs off-leash whenever possible to allow for more intense bounding and leaping exercise, there is no telling when they may discover a hidden treasure of putrid decomposition or bound into swampy area of decay. This necessitates seeking a clear brook or pond for optimal rinsing. Fortunately, our dogs need little prodding to prance into water, regardless of season or temperature. And most of the gross gook dissolves off their sleek hair. But depending on the depth and breadth of the disgusting detritus, outside hosing and bathing may still be required.

Whether Jesse is jogging or I am walking, our accompanying dogs dart vigorously in various directions, detectively guided by their scent-seeking noses. Overheated by overexertion, Tory, like Chelsea before her, will often collapse in the cooling solace of an inviting mud puddle. And there go my hopes of bringing home a minimally sullied spaniel. Although I rarely run at will, I will reluctantly sprint to encourage the dogs' chasing me and thus bypassing a potential puddle plopping. Tory's rust-colored legs and abdomen frequently bear unmistakable evidence of Jesse's jog at the neighboring sports field, prompting Tory's heat relief in rain-soaked remnants of baseball diamond clay.

We always keep dog towels accessible for wiping before house or car entry. But even clean dogs cloud car windows with nose prints and drool. In defense of personal cleanliness, I eventually banned our excitable canines from front car seats. Purchased restraining devices have kept dogs and their disdainful dirt in the back seat or way back of our progression of station wagons and SUVs.

Even while invisibly fenced within the confines of our property, our springers can still get into yucky stuff. There is no preventing a passing wild animal from leaving a particular appealing deposit—some yucky treasure that our dogs are as delighted to discover as much as I am disgusted to find smeared upon them.

Dogs and gardening applications are not always compatible. Chelsea annually indulged in her spring ritual of wallowing in pungent mulch, newly spread by gardeners throughout our yard. Even more distressing to me, young puppy Tory found delicious delight in organic fertilizer and slug deterrent. She chowed down on these garden products as if they were bacon bits, while ruining new plantings and mature hostas. Surprisingly, Tory was not sickened from her peculiar choices of delectables. But I was quite sick with worry over her behavior.

Yet another time puppy Tory did get sick. One night we upsettingly watched our eight-month-old pup wobble around the kitchen like a drunken sailor and collapse spastically onto the floor, appearing to suffer the effects of some disabling neurological disease. By morning Tory seemed back to her normal perky puppy self, but I still took her to our veterinary clinic for examination. The vet confirmed my suspicions of her ailment origin. Having had a very damp spring, there were many fungal varieties sprouting throughout our property. Curious Tory had likely ingested some "magic" mushroom that temporarily affected her nervous system.

We have no way to dissuade our dogs from their offensive attractions, whether they become sick or we are sickened by their horrible habits. We tolerate them because we are otherwise delighted by the more endearing attributes of our carousing canines. But undeniably, the yuck sucks!

Chapter 12

Sick as a Dog

Concerns about health care are ubiquitous in our contemporary society. Yet when we bring a furry bundle of irrepressible energy into our home, we rarely focus on either the short- or long-term health care ramifications of dog parenting.

We soon discover, however, that joys of dog ownership are unavoidably intertwined with the complications of dog health care. That naturally includes expected routine care of puppy shots, neutering, annual checkups, updating vaccinations, and administering preventive medications. But we are totally unprepared for the multitude of accidents and medical mishaps that befall our pets. And despite the quantity and diversity of illnesses and problems my husband and I have encountered in over almost sixty (many overlapping) years of dog parenting, I am amazed that concern for potential medical catastrophes never enters the otherwise thoughtful decision to bring another pet into our family. It just seems to come with the territory.

We first bought an Irish setter, a sporty dog, to accompany us on our sporty activities. Hiking with our happy hound in northern Arizona, among the Ponderosa pines of Flagstaff, Sedona, or the Apache White River reservation, was just what we imagined. Lance deliriously led the way but never ranged beyond visible or vocal contact. However, we lived in southern Arizona, in the Sonoran Desert, an expansive tract of cactus outback. We humans admired the stately saguaros, burgeoning barrel cactus, and the curvaceous prickly pears, but we quickly learned to give wide berth to the brittle, spiny-armed cholla. Aptly nicknamed the jumping cactus, the calamitous cholla shockingly relinquishes its barb-like thorns with minimal brushing of its prickly branches. But how do you explain that to a dog? Of course we didn't, and we couldn't. Before we recognized this dire desert hazard, poor Lance was multiply impaled by cholla's painful, porcupine-like quills. Lance's attempts to bite them off only made matters worse, as cholla spines lodged in his muzzle. At home, we individually extracted each painful needle from our thorn-pummeled pooch but sadly realized the impossibility of further desert hiking with free-ranging dogs.

Life in southern Arizona also afforded us the opportunity to venture across the Mexican border to the northeastern beaches of the Gulf of California. Crammed with camping and kayaking gear and our youthful dog Lance, we drove our red Jeep Commando to the popular beach of Puerto Peñasco, or Rocky Point. From our seaside campsite, Lance buoyantly swam after our kayak or toward dolphins offshore and ran exuberantly all over the sun-drenched sand. By our second day, however, Lance was venturing nowhere, unusually reluctant to stray from car or tent despite our encouragements to join us elsewhere. Was he sick or exhausted, we wondered. Was it too much heat or swimming in salt water?

Finally I realized that the sensitive webbed skin between Lance's toes had become painfully red and burnt from the prior day's beach running. Any additional steps on overheated sand created even further discomfort for our distressed dog. So now what to do, miles from the border and familiar American veterinary care? For a fairly new dog owner, I devised a creative solution: I dressed Lance's four legs in two pairs of Jesse's white cotton socks, securely tied above Lance's knees, giving our rusty-colored setter the appearance of a miniature thoroughbred racehorse. More importantly, Lance soon discovered he could continue cavorting on the blistering hot beach without further distress to his painful paws. So prematurely aborting our first Mexican beach camping trip was fortunately avoided.

As our precious puppy matured into a handsome setter, he sadly developed inexplicable hot spots. Irresistibly chewing on his itchy skin, Lance further created reddened, bald, and irritated patches. Our local vet in rural Casa Grande, accustomed to treating farm animals, first suspected mange and treated Lance accordingly. However, no oral or topical meds eliminated the problem. So our vet referred Lance to a specialist in Scottsdale, about fifty miles north. The distance did not deter us, as we were used to driving often to the Phoenix area for Lance's obedience training, Jesse's soccer practices and games, dining, and shopping.

As our family medical representative, Jesse took Lance to the specialist but was shocked by the seventy-five-dollar bill for examination and diagnostics. That doesn't sound like much now, but assuredly, it was actually a lot of money to us, a young couple in the mid-1970s.

"The dog only cost seventy-five dollars," Jesse complained to the vet. But as I later told Jesse, who never managed our finances, "What is the alternative? Are we going to abandon our darling dog over an expensive vet bill?" It would be great to say that the seventy-five dollars was money well spent and happily solved Lance's dermatology problems. But that was never the case. The actual origin of Lance's hot spots was never specifically identified. So Lance was treated for his idiopathic dermatitis with a course of oral and topical steroids to calm the inflammation and consequent itching. There were temporary improvements, but the problem never completely resolved. We spent a lot more money on stopgap meds to quell Lance's skin condition. Fortunately, as a surgical resident in the Boston area in the late 1970s, Jesse could legally obtain some free drug samples that minimized the expense of Lance's pharmaceutical needs. But sadly, we were constantly admonishing besieged Lance to stop biting and scratching his hot spots.

Sometimes owners are inadvertently the cause of animal illness. We owned a Jeep with four-wheel drive capability way before SUVs were ubiquitous in suburbia. So Jesse insisted on driving it over bumpy, off-road terrain in the Sedona red-rock area, even though there was plenty of spectacular scenery to be viewed from main roads. From rattling around in the back of the Jeep, both Irish setters regurgitated masses as rust-colored as the ubiquitous clay-infused environment. According to Jesse, they were sick from lapping up clay-soaked puddles. I did not accept that diagnosis, even though Jesse had the medical pedigree in our family. Lance and Brandy were more likely carsick from our tumultuous ride, I thought, tossing up semi-digested dog food, commercially reddened with food coloring.

Our domestic dogs might eat indiscriminately if left to their own devices, but that does not mean their sensitively evolved digestive systems can handle what they curiously consider edible. When springer Chelsea was new to our family, our teenage son Ben was also developing personal preferences about what he considered edible as well as attempting to cook his favorite foods. At Ben's request, I bought him the necessary ingredients to make lasagna, a popular dish that I had personally never attempted to bake. So I left Ben to his ingredients and cooking implements and avoided the kitchen—better to clean up the anticipated mess at the end than watch progressive stages of culinary calamity. Chelsea apparently was olfactorily oriented toward the kitchen commotion, and Ben was not particularly a vigilant mutt monitor. I have no idea how far along Ben was with his lasagna preparation when stealthy Chelsea ate two pounds of raw ground beef, but I do know that Ben was no part of the cleanup brigade that attended to Chelsea's massive diarrhea. Although canine ancestors likely filled their bellies with large raw hunks of hunted meat, our domesticated canines have apparently developed more refined stomachs that cannot tolerate an oversized portion of uncooked beef.

On another occasion, however, teenage Ben was subjected to the resultant gastric distress of his friend Sam's youthful dog Tally. Finding an unattended and seizable edible on the kitchen counter, the yellow Labrador retriever sneakily stole and ate an entire rising pizza dough. The boys had a hard time sleeping in Sam's room that night accompanied by Tally, whose malodorous flatulence from percolating yeast exploded exponentially overnight.

I can't even begin to enumerate how many times in my decades of dog ownership that I have sought veterinary advice about doggy indigestion and gastric disturbances. The first line of recommendation for the ailing dog is temporarily switching to a bland diet of boiled meat (usually hamburger) and white rice. So I never toss out leftover rice from Chinese takeout orders. Unmistakable trapezoidal cartons of boiled rice reside latently in our freezer for potential reconstitution into future bland diet demands.

In addition to dietary restrictions, many of the maladies that our dogs have developed require oral medications. Most are not particularly palatable, thus requiring surreptitious pill-intake strategies. My preferred process is a swift pilling maneuver: hold open the bottom jaw, insert pill far back in the throat, close jaw quickly, grasp both jaw and snout to prevent reopening, and immediately massage neck to induce swallowing. The minor negative consequence of somewhat offensive dog mouth smell on my fingers is easily removed by subsequent hand washing. But over a long course of meds or when Liza, for instance, had months of daily pills for various aging ailments, the dogs find their own strategies to thwart pill administration. Liza would preemptively chomp on my fingers to prevent the pill deposit in her throat. In the interest of hand preservation, I often reverted to plan B: peanut butter hors d'oeuvres. Although this requires a bit of preparation time, there is rarely a pill that doesn't get eaten if buried in a canapé of peanut butter atop a saltine cracker. The dogs tend to hover round as soon as the sweet smell of peanut butter wafts from the jar. So even if just one of two resident dogs is to be medicated, I minimize favoritism by supplying peanut butter treats for both. However, I am particularly careful to ensure that the ailing dog is the intended recipient of the medicinal canapé.

When sweet puppy Tory returned home post-op from recommended six-month-old spaying, she developed completely liquefied, squirting diarrhea. Although Tory was spayed at the optimal time for an appropriate reason, I still felt guilty about her subsequent distress. It seemed to be adding insult to injury to subject a perfectly healthy, happy pup to a major operation, which resulted thereafter in such upsetting intestinal distress. Bland diet and oral antibiotics fortunately returned Tory to her perky pre-op puppy persona.

In her youth, Tory created her own problems as well. She took an incorrigible interest in collecting rocks, of all shapes and sizes, and holding them in her mouth like prized possessions. With a gravel driveway and yard peppered with stones easily obtained with minimal surface scratching, there was no deterring Tory from her troublesome habit. By one year old, Tory curiously amassed a fort-like collection of unearthed rocks, logs from our woodpile, and selected fallen branches that she piled haphazardly on our backyard bluestone patio. Her rock fetish was particularly concerning. As Tory typically pounded her front paws at our sliding glass patio door to request house reentry, our housecleaner/pet sitter Vinny worried that she would crash into the door, rock in mouth, and shatter glass with grave injury to both door and herself. Fortunately, the glass was never smashed by Tory, who thankfully outgrew her rock collecting frequency as her destructive puppy teething habit also diminished.

But that's not to say young Tory's rock attraction was completely innocuous. One morning she inexplicably vomited right after eating breakfast. When Vinny arrived shortly thereafter for expected housecleaning, Tory peed a large puddle on the kitchen floor. It was a distinctly different stream from her typical excitement pee, which still dribbles out of her when she is so happy to see either of the important men in her life, Jesse or Vinny. Those two closely occurring, uncharacteristic episodes were sufficient for me to make an immediate vet appointment. And I was not without valid concern.

"Does she like to eat rocks?" asked our longtime vet, after external examination and gloved anal extraction of one small rock, which looked a lot like our gravel driveway pebbles.

"Yes, she does," I sheepishly admitted, feeling like a rather delinquent doggy mommy. "But I don't see how I can prevent her from doing that."

"I can also feel more rocks in her belly," Dr. Kyrka added, "so I think we should x-ray her." That necessitated sedation and leaving Tory at the Wayland Animal Clinic for several hours. The radiologic results confirmed a few more rocks in her digestive tract, but appearing small enough to hopefully pass without serious obstruction. Tory was released and prescribed the requisite bland diet. I, however, was assigned the ignominious task of examining bowel movements for rock expulsion.

"You can use these to test for rocks," said the vet, handing me several tongue depressors. More surprising joys of dog ownership. And yes, I was able to discern by tongue depressor, not going anywhere near anyone's tongue, that pebbles were perfunctorily passed. I was just glad that Tory never swallowed the baked potato-sized stones that she was often found hoarding.

Tory also contracted a nasty bout of diarrhea while accompanying us on her first summer vacation on Martha's Vineyard—one of the rare places that we take our dogs as they can drive with us to this special island getaway. We were upset for Tory but just as concerned about maintaining the cleanliness of the house and property we were borrowing from a generous friend. While never certain of the origin of intestinal distress, we supposed that Tory had been sickened by either gulping seawater while swimming to retrieve tennis balls or lapping from muddy puddles while accompanying our walks and jogs.

Whatever made young Tory sick fortunately did not affect Harry who was also with us. But Harry, who had vacationed many summers on the Vineyard, had not always left unscathed from his place of birth. The most traumatic event resulted from his tangling with a wild turkey. As reported to me by Jesse returning from a jog, our bird dog Harry instinctively chased after a troop of turkey chicks. Not surprisingly, the mother turkey retaliated. And who could blame her for protecting her chick progeny? Harry was the big bad wolf. And he suffered the consequences.

We did not recognize the problematic situation until two days later when Harry was acting uncharacteristically subdued and shivering in the hot sun. Upon inspection, I found a leg wound, presumably from mother turkey pecking. From our combined medical and dog ownership experience, we surmised that turkey beak bacteria had created a systemic infection. Harry was very sick! We immediately contacted a Vineyard veterinary clinic and announced Harry's problem. They seemed skeptical about our diagnosis, having not encountered other cases of turkey-pecked canines. Yet we doubted Harry could have been the first as the MVY wild turkey population was significant. Nevertheless, Harry's infection was obvious, and he was treated immediately with intravenous antibiotics and more oral meds to follow. Hooray for the miracle of antibiotics, which saved Harry from possible demise by turkey tangling and similarly vanquished countless other potentially debilitating illnesses contracted by our active family canines.

Dog-loving parasites have contributed to a notable number of other pressing problems. In our early days of dog ownership, monthly applications of tick and flea deterrent were not available. So, I had to deal with infestations as they inopportunely occurred. Finding an engorged rubbery tick embedded in our dog's furry body is always unpleasant, but I have become rather cavalier about picking them off and either burning or flushing the objectionable bloodsuckers. The topical preventive products are not completely tick-proof, however, as I still occasionally encounter a parasitic adherent while caressing my canines. Even worse is the discovery of an errant creepy crawler in our bed, or on our own people bodies. But for the most part, prescribed veterinary products like Advantix® or Frontline®, and other similar commercially available applications, have greatly reduced the amount of invasive danglers.

Years gone by, we were mainly concerned about unwelcome wood ticks. But over time our worried attention has focused more on the diminutive deer tick, host to dreaded Lyme disease, debilitating to both dogs and people, and increasingly prevalent with increase of the local deer population. Despite the threat of potential disease, the presence of deer on our property is always exciting to both me and our dogs, albeit for different reasons. I love to view the aesthetically graceful, white-tailed ungulates. Instinctually, the springers want to chase after them.

While my use of parasite prevention products was predominantly applied to fend off the preponderance of ticks in our woodsy Boston suburbs, we also benefitted greatly from the flea deterrent properties. I have vividly upsetting memories from earlier decades of discovering distressing flea infestations, when dogs were found scratching excessively. Although people are not flea hosts, the little buggers will still bite enticing human bodies—a potentially realistic hazard with dogs sleeping in our beds.

Bathing our dogs and laundering canine and people bedding was not enough to eliminate fleas, however. There was no telling where fleas had invaded our indoor sanctuary, in carpeting or on dog-permitted couches and mattresses. Vacuuming could not ensure complete removal either. The sure-fire elimination process was to bomb the house with a self-releasing aerosol can of toxic flea pesticide. Before spray onset, all humans and pets had to flee the house and remain evacuated for at least two hours. Thorough house airing was necessitated upon return. The fumigation process was indeed effective, but engineering this military operation in consideration of human and animal occupants was complicated and exhausting. And I had to fight this flea battle on multiple fronts, in defense of Lance and Brandy in our little Wellesley house and later in "flea-migating" Liza and Chelsea in our first Weston domicile. Only later did I recognize that topical tick deterrent fortuitously freed me from formidable flea eradication as well. I have never had to bomb our current Weston home of fifteen years, and hopefully the benefits have far outweighed potential negative side effects of multiple months of applied pesticide.

But admittedly, the tick deterrent is not 100 percent effective. Some sneaky ticks seem to hang on longer than others before they are overcome by pesticide-infused dog skin. And when some ticks do take hold, they present potential disease-born consequences.

So when three-year-old springer Harry abnormally would not stand and was favoring a very sore front leg, Jesse had to take him to weekend emergency veterinary services in my absence. Well aware of our tick-laden environment, I suggested that Jesse inquire about Lyme disease, which is known to affect joints. After radiology and blood tests for multiple ailments and $800 later, guess what was Harry's problem? Just what had I thought, Lyme disease. Once again, Jesse was somewhat jokingly reluctant to pay a veterinary bill that was almost twice the cost of Harry's original purchase price. He even voiced that opinion in the waiting room to less-than-sympathetic listeners. Of course, I was no more pleased with the unfortunately high veterinary charges, but I was not about to abandon Harry for a more impressive fiscal balance sheet.

Antibiotics were prescribed, and Harry improved rapidly. We were glad to learn that Lyme disease in dogs was more easily diagnosed and amenable to treatment than its parallel illness in people. Nevertheless, since Harry's disturbing bout with Lyme disease, all our springers are vaccinated annually for this tick-born disease—a small, preventive price to pay.

But we also learned through longtime dog ownership experience that Lyme disease is not the only illness that ticks can inflict on dogs. As mentioned before, I took Tory to the vet when she temporarily exhibited behavior that seemed like neurological impairment. Our vet suspected the disrupting culprit might be mushroom toxicity. But, to be thorough, he ordered a panel of blood tests to screen for a range of tick-borne illnesses. And they found one, which was unfamiliar to me. Tory was diagnosed with Anaplasma, identified by a low blood platelet count, which was incidentally unrelated to her probable mushroom ingestion and temporary neurological imbalance—a lucky find, one might say, to be able to identify this disease in its early stages and treat with antibiotics before Tory became symptomatic.

Our dogs have also had a variety of traumatic accidents necessitating emergency veterinary care. One afternoon I received a distressed phone call at work from my kids. Liza had returned from her neighborhood wanderings with a blood-soaked abdomen. I flew out of the local newspaper office and drove home as fast as I could without incurring a speeding ticket or accident. Frightened to fully inspect Liza's gory injury, I wrapped her bloody body in towels, put her in the back of our station wagon, and sped directly to the Weston Veterinary Clinic. What had probably happened, according to the vet, was that Liza had caught her underbelly on some kind of wires or fencing and ripped the skin off her abdomen to extract herself from the unintentional snaring. Many worries, stitches, and antibiotics later, she recovered amazingly well.

When Harry was six years old, he had two traumatic episodes to the same front foot within a few months. He inexplicably broke a toenail quite close to the quick, followed by a slashing cut across a footpad. Both very painful situations required veterinary attention and antibiotic follow-up. Most difficult to manage were directions to keep the bandaged foot clean and dry on a dog who prefers to spend much of his time pounding the great outdoors. Although Harry resiliently recovered from both foot problems, his attitude toward the veterinary clinic changed dramatically from then on. He's no longer the happy-go-lucky hound at veterinary visits, cheerfully sniffing all the exciting animal and clinic smells. Ever since his successive paw accidents, traumatized Harry has planted himself as close as possible to me even for routine appointments, pitifully shaking by my side.

When I bring any of our dogs for an annual routine veterinary check, I know better than to end the appointment by saying, "See you next year." Invariably, some medical incident will return us to the vet well in advance of the next annual checkup.

Chapter 13

Ten Thousand-Dollar Dog

Although Harry was beset by a variety of health concerns in his youth, I did not particularly consider him any more illness- or accident-prone than any other of our family dogs. That is until he was almost ten years old, when he went through an expensive, eighteen-month spate of medical crises. And that's how hapless Harry eventually became our $10,000 dog.

The series of crises began when I returned from a 2009 Mother's Day visit to extended family in Boca Raton, Florida. Longtime pet sitter Vinny, having also become our airport driver, gave me the dog report on our half-hour drive home from Boston's Logan Airport. Harry had been just fine for the several days we were away (Jesse had been with me briefly in Boca, squeezed in between business trips to Venezuela and Japan). But on the day I was returning, Vinny related, Harry had seemed unusually subdued and was not interested in eating. Harry never had the biggest appetite for his standard dry dog food, but the lack of activity in our typically raring-to-go-at-any-time dog immediately seemed cause for concern. Harry had been limping and favoring his left hind leg when overexercised that spring, so I wondered whether that was contributing to the current problem in our aging springer.

Anxiously greeting Harry as soon as I arrived home that evening, I noticed he was drooling—definitely not a good sign. And on cursory exam, Harry was reluctant to open his mouth, and his neck was swollen—more telltale symptoms not to be ignored. From more than fifty-five years of sporty dog ownership, I had learned that a small stick or even a blade of grass could get caught in the back of a dog's throat and disrupt the salivary glands with resultant infection and swelling.

I kept an overnight watch on Harry, occasionally forcing some water down his throat for hydration. Not surprising to me, Harry was no better in the morning, so we went to our familiar Wayland Animal Clinic. Dr. Terry Purbaugh, with capable staff assistant hands, was able to pry open and examine Harry's mouth and throat for assessment.

"Harry has a fairly big wound under his tongue," Dr. Purbaugh told me, "which we have attempted to clean out as best we can." Of course, we didn't know how Harry was wounded, but I was not completely shocked by his injury, considering the objects that might find their way into Harry's mouth. Harry was not prone to carrying rocks and sticks in his mouth like Tory did, but he was obsessed with retrieving tennis balls. Eventually, any ball he chased became slimy with saliva, forming a sticky coating to which bits of dirt and vegetation would filthily adhere.

I appreciatively paid the ninety-three-dollar bill, and Harry was discharged with a two-week course of antibiotics.

And through the miraculous wonder drugs of modern science, Harry improved impressively. That is, until he didn't. About ten days off antibiotics, drooling and throat swelling recurred. According to Jesse, a quite knowledgeable and respected people surgeon, Harry's non-healing throat infection was likely due to the undiscovered object that had originally punctured Harry's mouth.

So we went back to our vets, who took Harry to surgery, opening Harry's neck externally under anesthesia, to more fully clean and drain his throat abscess, and further search for the culprit of the calamity.

"There was quite a lot of swelling and abscessed tissue," Dr. Robert Kyrka reported, "but we did not find anything specific lodged in Harry's throat." However, Dr. Kyrka also acknowledged, "Foreign bodies are not easy to find, and they can even travel internally to be lodged somewhere else in your dog. Hopefully, the deep cleaning of all the abscessed tissue will be enough to promote healing. But we can't be sure until we see how he responds."

Poor Harry was discharged with an Elizabethan collar to prevent scratching his shaved, sliced-open, and sutured-back-together neck, and of course, with a two-week course of antibiotics. I appreciatively paid the $640 bill.

At home I initially gave Harry the opportunity to be collar-free and saw that he did not seem inclined to scratch at his surgical wound. But without the collar, the wound was not protected by other outside interference, specifically Tory's preference to nuzzle near as possible to her "big brother." So the collar was re-attached to avoid puppy licking and ensure optimal wound healing.

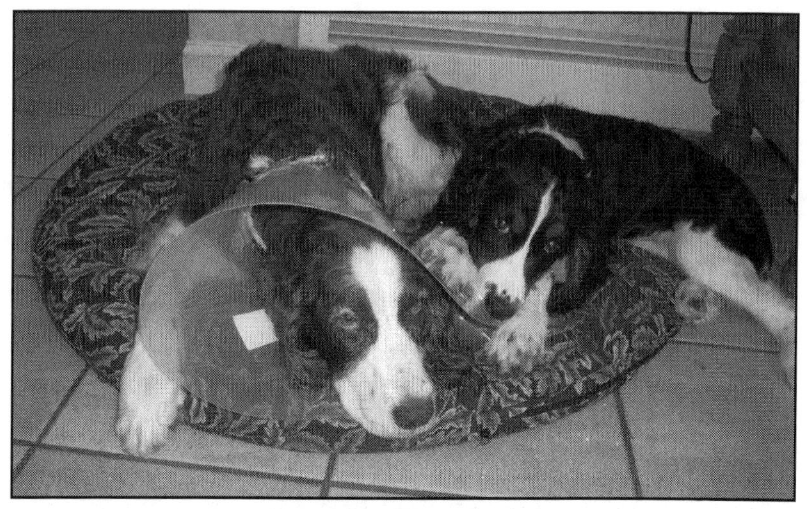

Protecting Harry's neck

Post-op, Harry could not be let loose in our yard and had to be leash-walked—less activity for Harry and more exercise for me, just about the time when my "involun-Tory" puppy diet exercise activities were somewhat diminishing.

All those antibiotics calmed Harry's throat infection, and he seemed on the happy road to recovery. That is, for about a month, as some draining persisted from his neck incision, and the swelling was never completely eliminated. "You're going to need a specialist, a veterinary surgeon," Dr. Kyrka informed me, referring us to Dr. John Benson at Vetcision, a veterinary specialty care center in nearby Waltham.

Dr. Benson examined Harry at our $145-consultation appointment and explained how he would surgically explore Harry more completely, without any promise of finding the originally offending object.

"Harry has been limping a lot lately," I also mentioned to Dr. Benson. "Dr. Kyrka said Harry needs to be anesthetized to take diagnostic x-rays. So, can you take them when he'll be anesthetized for his throat surgery?" I inquired.

Without missing a beat, Dr. Benson leaned over to externally examine Harry's left hind leg. "We don't need x-rays," he told me. "I know what's wrong with him. He has a torn ACL." Then Dr. Benson told me about his preferred operation for cruciate ligament repair, called tibial plateau leveling osteotomy (TPLO). He provided a printed description detailing the problem, the surgical treatment which involves cutting the tibia to realign the leg, and an estimate of $3,600 for the surgical repair—something to consider after Harry's throat operation.

On July 2, Harry's ailing neck was once again opened up and explored. Due to Jesse's and my prior travel plans, Vinny accommodatingly brought Harry home the next day, with drains in his neck and a glass vial with Dr. Benson's fortuitous finding, a one-inch piece of wood about the width of a straw. When I brought Harry back to Vetcision for drain removal the following week, Dr. Benson told me, "The wood chunk wasn't easy to locate amid all the internal neck folds. We're really lucky that I got it out." Personally, I thought there was more than luck. I credited our talented vet surgeon.

The piece of wood looked a lot like the countless other small wood pieces that composed the garden mulch that was spread in spring. I guessed that the wood chunk that punctured under Harry's tongue and hid in the internal folds of his throat had found its way there by adhering to a saliva-slimed tennis ball. So I appreciatively paid the $1,942 surgery bill, which brought the total tally for vet attention for the throat wound to $2,820. Harry came home with more instructions about how he needed to be contained, necessitating more attentiveness and doggy exercising by me.

At that point I was in no hurry to subject Harry or our bank account to the TPLO operation to repair his torn cruciate ligament. Nevertheless, I discussed the concern with Dr. Kyrka. Before the more recently developed TPLO, he explained, the traditional treatment, still in use, has been the lateral suture technique, somewhat less expensive but perhaps more prone to future rupture in active dogs. With either operation there would be a fairly long recuperative period during which Harry could not leave the house unleashed. Harry would have to be accompanied outdoors at all times, from early morning to late at night.

Given our fairly frequent travel schedule, I was as much concerned about monitoring the recuperative period as putting Harry through the operation. And having recovered from the lengthy saga of his throat wound, Harry was finally resuming his seemingly cheerful, active life, albeit sometimes on only three legs. My admonishments to Jesse about overexercising Harry were fairly futile. Jesse only has one gear, fast-forward, and Harry would not be left behind.

However, throughout autumn Harry was becoming more lame and less willing to exert any pressure on his left rear leg. An operation seemed inevitable, but we had some decisions to make. So I wrote an inquiry e-mail to a Swiss surgical colleague of Jesse, Dr. Jörg Auer. Both doctors have extensive experience in musculoskeletal surgery, but Joerg's has always been with animal patients. Here's what I wrote to our veterinarian friend:

Hello Jörg,

I am writing to ask your opinion about how to treat our dog who has a torn ACL on his left hind leg. We have finally decided on surgery but the question is which type:

(traditional) lateral suture or (cutting edge) tibial plateau leveling osteotomy.

Here's some background info: Harry is an active 10 year-old English springer spaniel, weighing about 50 pounds. He is a taller than average springer but he is rather slim and bony these days. He has had the tear for several months. He was limping occasionally in the spring & summer, but now he is almost a 3-legged dog. Although he does not appear to be in major discomfort, from anything we can tell behaviorally, from his condition. He still wants to run around all over and chase balls. He loves to run with Jesse or me when we take him out. And we have a new young female springer spaniel, 9 months old, who has been keeping him very active (I hope her presence in our family since April did not contribute to Harry's ACL tear, but I guess I will never know the answer to that.)

If you are wondering why we have taken so long to come to this decision, Harry was originally diagnosed for his ACL tear by a vet surgeon when he was operated on in July, due to a festering wound in his mouth which had been a continuing saga since May. Fortunately, the surgeon was able to find the piece of wood which pierced under his tongue and got lodged somewhere in the soft tissues. So we were "recuperating" from 2 months of mouth wound caretaking and surgeries. Then we were hesitant to put Harry thru a major surgery if not necessary. Jesse was reticent about this too. And we were traveling intermittently. Now it seems like Harry his holding his hind leg up most of the time, so the surgery appears to be necessary.

Here's what I know already: the diagnosing vet is very keen on TPLO. He thinks it is a much better technique than lateral suture with more lasting results. Our regular vet thinks we could go either way, but observes that the TPLO is a much more invasive surgery due to the cutting of the tibia.

Money is not the most pressing factor but TPLO will cost about $1000 (not an insignificant amount) more than the lateral suture operation (about $3600 vs about $2600).

I am concerned about recuperation because nobody likes to lay low around here, not Harry, Jesse or the puppy. I will have to be holding all of them down. So I'm wondering if one or the other of these operations might have any quicker recuperation.

Thanks for reading this long e-mail. If you have some opinion, advice, or suggestions, I would like to hear from you.

Best wishes, Beryl

Reminding us that he is an equine veterinary surgeon, Jörg kindly forwarded my e-mail to Dr. Rico Vannini, a Swiss small animal vet colleague, who responded extensively to my concerns via Jörg.

lieber Jörg,
In my opinion TPLO is the way to go. Doing it for 12 years by now, it is still the most effective technique in my hands. Even if the dog is 10 years old, he has a good chance to completely recover. The dogs return faster to normal activity and there is no risk of suture failure, which is very common in large breed dogs after the classical lateral suture technique.

Clinical experience shows clearly that the majority of dogs return to normal full function.
Important factor for success is, of course, the experience of the surgeon doing the procedure. After surgery the dog

needs 6 weeks of leash walks and another 6 weeks with no explosive activities. After 3 months everything has healed and the dog can go back to his regular activity. The major problem owners usually have with the operated dogs is to keep them quiet, especially when they start to feel frisky again.

Hope to have helped a little

Best wishes
Rico

Of course, we were not going to bring Harry to Switzerland for an operation. Fortunately, our Swiss veterinary advisors referred us to a colleague at nearby Tufts School of Veterinary Medicine, Dr. Randy Boudrieau. Jesse happened to know Randy as well through their international musculoskeletal research association.

Enormously appreciating the ease of e-mail contacts, I forwarded the prior communications to Dr. Boudrieau and added the following:

> What is of major concern to me is the lengthy recuperative period. We also have a very active young springer (just 10 months), so I understand I will have to keep them totally separated for some time. Additionally, we travel a lot, so this recuperative period will be a lot more difficult for our pet sitter to handle.
>
> Maybe there is a place Harry can go for dog rehab? (sort of joking here but not totally.) Thank you for your assistance as we try to make these decisions.

We appreciated Dr. Boudrieau's prompt responsiveness to our surgical decision-making inquiry. Here is most of what he wrote on November 16, 2009:

Dear Beryl:
Sorry to hear about your "pup" and the issues...your note certainly has been around the world!!
Anyway, I know both Jörg and Rico well, and of course I know Jesse...Bottom line, I agree with Rico 100%. He summarized everything very nicely. As far as your concern about which procedure to choose—and the recuperation—my choice would remain the TPLO (by the way, John Benson was also one of our surgical residents a few years ago as well). I am not in favor of a lateral suture technique for an active dog in the first place, but it is a popular procedure.
With a TPLO, we are changing the functional stresses around the knee (eliminating anterior tibiofemoral shear forces in extension)—thus basically eliminating the need for the cruciate ligament.
Therefore, our only concern in the postoperative period is the healing of the osteotomy. There is still the 6-8 weeks of strict exercise restriction postoperatively (this is a healing fracture), but then a gradual return to full activity (assuming that the fracture has progressed appropriately) over the next 3-4 weeks, and that's it. So basically back to full activity in 1/2 the time. In addition, since there is no restriction on joint motion (as opposed to the lateral suture), the dogs are much more comfortable much sooner postoperatively... the TPLO will usually be placing weight on the limb within a day or two, whereas the lateral suture will be very reluctant to do so for a couple of weeks. Lastly, as Rico described,

the ultimate functional result will be very good, and in my opinion as well, much better than the lateral suture. Yes, the TPLO is a more invasive procedure than the lateral suture, but the more rapid recovery, greater comfort and better functional result make this the better choice in my opinion. As far as postoperative care, the TPLO also is easier, as there is less to worry about—stronger and more stable fixation—but the early restriction remains important, as this is a healing fracture. The dog will feel good enough, very quickly, to want to do more than I would want, so this is the main concern. The latter is easily controlled by confining indoors and outside only on a leash long enough to eliminate, and that's it. No running/jumping or unrestrained activity outside or in the house—for example, up & down stairs. As far as your other dog, no playing/rough-housing. When you're at home I would think you could control all these activities fairly easily; when you're out, a crate (large enough for the dog to easily stand and turn around) ensures no silly activity.
So, if this was my dog, I would not hesitate to do the TPLO, even in an older dog, for all the reasons above. I'm happy to chat with you if you'd like...but if you'd like to move forward, please call our surgical liaison. We have a couple of openings this week.

Best regards,
Randy

Well, that settled it. I had received the best expert advice I could hope for. Both Harry and I were ready for surgery. I made the appointment for Harry to see Dr. Boudrieau at Tufts University Foster Hospital for Small Animals in

Grafton on a November Tuesday and ended up leaving Harry for TPLO surgery of his left hind leg for the next day.

Surgery went well, and Jesse departed later that day for a prearranged meeting in Madrid. I was pleased to receive daily post-op telephone updates from Dr. Boudrieau's surgical team. In Harry's absence, Tory surprisingly and quickly replaced Harry as our newspaper delivery dog.

Friday was pickup day. A somewhat subdued Harry was released to me along with his treatment report, outlining the procedures taken and personally concluding, "Thank you for bringing Harry to Tufts; he is a very sweet dog." After appreciatively paying the bill of $3,210, I took home Harry, along with his discharge papers, which included a very detailed list of patient care instructions.

"Exercise restriction and good nursing care," I read, "are paramount to a successful, uncomplicated recovery." Believe me, considering the expense and time to be invested in Harry, I intended to carefully comply with post-op expectations to ensure Harry's optimal surgical recovery and long-term prognosis.

Specifics were delineated as follows: "COMPLETE exercise restriction is critical for the next eight to ten weeks. Harry should be confined to a crate or small area and only taken on short leash walks outside to urinate and defecate. Absolutely no running, jumping, stairs climbing, long leash walks, or unsupervised activity should be allowed."

And if that wasn't specific enough, the discharge instructions further warned me: "Failure to adhere to these guidelines may result in a slower-than-normal recovery or complications that could require additional treatment or surgery."

We owned a reasonably sized, attractive wooden crate, used during Tory's growing puppyhood, which I centrally positioned in the kitchen and filled with comfortable bedding. Although the instructions and restrictions rationale were crystal clear to me, no one seemed to have read Harry the memo. My contrarily caged canine was completely distraught. He would not settle down to even notice whether the bedding was comfortable. He just stood behind the bars, distressfully barking. Worried about his continuous standing on his newly operated leg, I soon realized I needed to rethink how Harry should be contained.

Plan B: I blocked off about a six-by-six-foot area of my office, allowing visibility into the kitchen by gate enclosure across the door opening. I also covered the carpeting with blankets and towels both for comfort and to catch any potential oozing discharge from the operative area. "If a small room is elected," directed the written restrictions, "he should not be able to jump up on or off furniture." I thought I had fulfilled that obligation within the space I had prepared, but I soon discovered I had not thoroughly anticipated Harry's reactions.

I sent this e-mail to Jesse:

> I picked Harry up this afternoon. He was very smiley and happy to go home. Most of his operated leg is shaved (a bit like a one-sided poodle cut). Very nice-looking incision on the inside. He is not licking at it so does not have to wear the Elizabethan collar. So since we have been home, a little over an hour, I am following directions about keeping him in a small area. He hated being kept in the crate, so now he is in the front of my office. But most of the

> time he has been whining about being closed in, even if I am at my desk. Well, this is going to be a challenge.

While I was working in my office, Harry finally settled down. But as soon as I left the office, unhappy Harry stood to object to his confinement, barking out his discontent. Worse than that, Harry managed to pleadingly plant his front legs up on my thirty-inch-high filing cabinets, creating further pressure on his rear operated leg. Was Harry ever going to relax, I wondered. Wouldn't the prescribed opioid Tramadol pill finally make him drowsy enough to lie down and sleep? I already felt unsuccessful at fulfilling the primary goals of "exercise restriction and good nursing care for uncomplicated recovery."

His intentionally un-bandaged surgical wound was looking more red and swollen to me, but admittedly I had not studied it so much initially to have a valid comparison over the course of several hours.

Plan C: I gated Harry into a small space in the kitchen, lined with comfy dog beds and towels and little possibility of rearing up on his hind legs. When Tory and I tried to sleep that night in my bedroom adjacent to the kitchen, Harry continued his plaintive protesting from his imprisoned partition. I periodically returned to him, wearily attempting to assuage his unrelenting distress. But Harry absolutely would not relax in his place of confinement. I finally called Jesse (when early morning for him in Madrid) to describe our hellish night at home. At that point, Jesse recommended my allowing Harry to join me and Tory in bed, although I was concerned both for Harry's injuring his leg by jumping out of the bed when I was sleeping and for oozing bloody discharge onto our bedding.

So I piled many absorbent towels on top of our bedding and was about to assist Harry onto our bed, as the mail-ordered portable staircase had yet to arrive. But, as I was organizing the logistics, anxious Harry leapt onto the bed before I could restrain him, so eager to access his preferred sleeping environment. And not surprisingly, after so many hours of distressful imprisonment, Harry instantaneously fell into deep sleep upon entering bedtime nirvana.

At eight thirty a.m. I sent a semi-relieved e-mail to Jesse:

> we all slept pretty much from 4:30 to 7:30
> the last hour has been a challenge, starting from getting Harry off bed, walking dogs, letting Tory get newspaper, feeding dogs, separating dogs, figuring out where to keep Harry, cleaning dog poop off my shoes, as it's hard to see where there's poop in the yard due to leaves all over ground.
> right now Harry is back in the front of my office while I am at the computer.
> at least he is sitting on his bed and not whining. wrote too fast. he is up again and not too thrilled to be contained.
> this is going to be rough!!

Around Saturday at noon, I sent the following e-mail to Dr. Boudrieau, attaching photos that I took of Harry's operated leg. We all know how a picture is worth a thousand words.

Hello Randy,
I picked Harry up Friday afternoon, and I became concerned about increasing discoloration of his skin by Friday evening, which seemed more bruised than when I picked

him up. It does, however, appear to be about the same this morning as last night. There is a lot of redness from the knee down and some purple discoloration on the inside below the hock.

The staples are in place, there is no draining, and there does not appear to be too much swelling. Again, no particularly noticeable changes from last night to this morning.

Admittedly, I was having a very hard time with him yesterday and last night about keeping him restrained in a small area. He was very distressed and standing up a lot, constantly tried to exit his confinement, likely putting more pressure on his hind legs than would be good for him.

I read and reread all the discharge instructions and what to look for. The paperwork said to call if I had ANY questions. So I spoke with animal hospital emergency last night and the attendant suggested I take his temperature, which I did, and he was not running a fever (so likely no infection).

On the functional side, since he has been home, he has eaten, defecated, drank a lot of water (I think because he was panting so much yesterday and last night from distress), and urinated numerous times. He is finally resting this morning, after many hours of crying last night.

I have given him the Rimadyl for inflammation as prescribed, and last evening I gave one pill of Tramadol when I was worried that he was jumping around in his confined area and may have injured his surgery.

Attached are some photos that I took last night & this morning.

My usual in-house surgeon is in Madrid, although we have been e-mailing, and I spoke with him early this morning after a rather sleepless night.

Basically, I really do not know if I am being overly concerned or whether I will be remiss in not going back to have someone see him today.
Thanks for your help.
Beryl

I heard back from Dr. Boudrieau on Saturday evening.

Dear Beryl:
Hopefully I can put your mind at ease...it is not unusual that we see some bruising. As long as there's no drainage—and he feels good (eating) then I would not worry. Also, the fact that he doesn't have a fever supports that there probably are no issues. Typically, it IS hard to restrain them as they are pretty comfortable on the leg very early on.
RE the photos, yes, there's a fair amount of bruising and some swelling. It is much more obvious on Harry because the areas are in the white skin/hair region...too bad his pigmented skin doesn't include the leg! It does look a bit nasty from a layperson's viewpoint (and I'll admit I'd also rather not see it), but all the bruising is a result of the surgical procedure—that is very obvious due to his light skin color. Also, from my perspective, it doesn't look too bad/concerning. Let me know if it worsens...I suspect the bruising will remain the same, but it would not surprise me if the swelling increased a bit.
Hope this helps!
Randy

I greatly appreciated our vet surgeon's responsiveness to my worries over Harry and told him so in one more e-mail:

Randy,
Thank you so much for your e-mail response. You have really made me feel better re Harry. He has generally calmed down today (compared to last night's distress), but he is still intermittently out of sorts about his restrictions. Since I wrote to you at midday, his leg seems to look about the same tonight. But it does seem to me that he is more reluctant to bear weight on it today than yesterday. For example, yesterday he quickly managed on his own our 3-4 stairs into the house. Today he seems to wait till I boost him. And when he is out walking on his leash, he mostly keeps his operated leg up in the air, whereas yesterday he seemed to have touched it down more. I would guess that when he was just released from the hospital yesterday, he may have tried to support himself more, and today is more sore from that.
But generally I think your e-mail reply has eased my mind as of now.
Goodnight. Beryl

I finally gave in to Harry's more vocal objections about indoor restrictions, allowing him to ambulate as usual throughout the ground floor of our house. As stipulated, I blocked Harry from climbing a full set of stairs to the second floor and Jesse's office, ordinarily a favorite place where the dogs hang out when Jesse is home. I watched out for Tory's exuberant attempts to playfully engage Harry. We initially carried Harry onto our bed at night and tried to prevent his jumping off in the morning. When the portable three-step staircase arrived, we patiently taught Harry to use this gentler method for bed entry and exit rather than his prohibited leap up or down. Outings were entirely on leash for two cold and snowy months. The necessities of walking Harry from morning to night were keeping me just as exercised as the puppy diet. Thankfully, Jesse often managed Harry's earliest morning activities with my firm insistence about being leashed outside at all times—no exceptions, as premature pressure on Harry's healing leg could further prolong his recovery.

Carrying out post-op instructions

Over time Harry appeared to be hitting the expected recovery marks outlined on the discharge papers: some amount of leg weight bearing about a week after surgery, weight bearing 50 percent of the time by two to four weeks, and continuing to improve slowly thereafter.

January 19, 2010, was judgment day. I brought Harry back to Tufts for x-rays and his two-month post-op appointment. Good news: recovery was proceeding well. Showing me the x-rays, Dr. Boudrieau observed that surgically cut bone to realign Harry's leg was healing very well and was about 70 percent grown back together—appropriate for this stage of his recuperation. I cheerfully thanked Harry's doctor and appreciatively paid our follow-up appointment bill of $290.

The next step was to gradually return Harry to normal activity level over one more month at which point he should be fully healed, back to running with Jesse, and chasing tennis balls to his heart's content. How to accomplish the *gradually* part was something of trial and error, and I wanted to avoid as much of the error, if possible. On his first unleashed day, Harry seemed initially hesitant, but he eventually resumed his usual morning routine of sniffing and scoping out our property, discovering the lingering scents of nocturnal creatures. Watching warily from inside, I let Harry loose for short time periods, calling him indoors if he got too frisky. For a few more weeks, we walked a fine line of giving Harry his physical freedom but minimizing overexertion.

We were just about out of the post-op "woods" for our now $6,000 dog when the next crisis arose. And it didn't have anything to do with his musculoskeletal system. On the Friday that was just three days after Harry's follow-up appointment, Jesse and I left for our prearranged ski vacation in Colorado. With Harry unleashed, Vinny was back to supposedly routine pet sitting. But by Saturday morning we heard from Vinny that Harry was ill with vomiting and diarrhea. To what could that be attributed? Might he have caught something at the recent trip to the animal hospital?

I also had another theory. The day before we left was January 21, Tory's first birthday. From the pet area of my regular grocery store, I had obtained a commercial pack of two flavor-stuffed dog chew bones, a first-time purchase for a birthday treat. Although I realize that birthday is not a concept that dogs actually grasp, I still like to celebrate with our pets by giving them both some special food or treat. The birthday girl did not get sick, but I wondered if Harry might have wolfed down chunks of his bone that were too large and internally abrasive.

Although Vinny was attentively trying to nurse Harry through the weekend until our usual veterinary clinic would be open, Harry's gastrointestinal distress worsened with episodes of bloody diarrhea. Vinny judiciously chose to take Harry to emergency veterinary services very late Sunday night.

On Monday morning I spoke with attending veterinarian Dr. Bari Spielman who said that Harry had been very sick upon admission. Although I offered my suspicions about the stuffed chew bone, the origin of Harry's severe gastroenteritis was never clear. Blood work and abdominal x-rays did not reveal any major abnormalities. Given intravenous fluids, medications to settle his stomach and TLC, Harry improved immensely and was released on Tuesday. I appreciatively gave my credit card number for the $2,200 bill, and Vinny brought Harry home with specific discharge directions for medication and feeding. Wrote Dr. Spielman: "Please limit Harry's activity to short leash walks for the next couple days." So much for Harry's short-lived freedom, post-TPLO surgery recuperation.

"Harry was a very good boy," added Dr. Spielman in the discharge notes. "We hope he continues to do well and is feeling as good as new over the next few days." And he did. By the time Jesse and I returned from our week away, Harry was completely back to normal. I couldn't say the same for poor Vinny, however, who had to heroically deal with all of Harry's trauma and recovery restrictions.

So we tallied over $8,000 for nine months of medical care, but who was counting? And Harry managed to be footloose and crisis-free for the next nine months, also giving us a bit of time to replenish our bank account.

When Jesse and I returned at the end of October 2010 from Jesse's ten-day medical teaching trip in Thailand, we were picked up by our reliable airport driver/pet sitter with a sadly familiar dog report. "All was perfectly fine," Vinny told us, "until today, when Harry hasn't seemed like his usual energetic, ball-chasing self. And he's not eating or drinking."

That did not sound good at all. And it was Sunday. Upon entering our house, I took one look at Harry's drooling face, felt his very swollen neck, and realized we could not wait for our local vet clinic's Monday morning opening. Despite being very tired and very jet-lagged after thirty-six hours of continuous traveling, I needed to take Harry to emergency veterinary services ASAP.

"I'll go too, if you want," Jesse said supportively.

"I really appreciate your offer," I said, "but you have to get up early for work tomorrow, and I don't. I'll take him." And I did.

Arriving about six p.m., with symptoms of excessive salivation, swollen neck, and fever of 104 degrees, Harry was examined and admitted to undergo a sedated oral exam and other indicated diagnostic procedures. Wearily, I went home.

Veterinarian Dr. Francesca Maffezzoli called me at about nine thirty p.m. Harry's fever had increased to 105 degrees, she reported, and he had a very high white blood cell count indicative of infection. Otherwise, no abscess or abnormality was discovered. She kept him in the hospital for supportive care, including pain management, anti-inflammatories, antibiotics, and intravenous fluids, to which he responded positively. On Monday, more tests: neck ultrasound, which showed a mass around the thyroid and nearby tissue; a needle biopsy to analyze cells for potential tumor pathology; chest x-ray that was negative; and blood work, which was generally within normal limits.

"Did you see any mouth wound?" I inquired, relating Harry's prior year's bout with the piercing stick that lodged in his throat. Despite quite similar presenting symptoms, this time there was no wound to be found.

Harry improved enough to go home by Monday evening. I just had to appreciatively pay the $1,800 bill, which officially made poor Harry our $10,000 dog in an eighteen-month period.

Harry was released with more meds to take and many discharge instructions with more caretaking work for me. For example: "Apply alternating warm and cold compresses to the swollen area of the neck three to four times daily for about ten minutes." Within the next few days, the remaining test results returned negative. There was no tumor. Harry was ill from an infection of unknown origin. But fortunately, he steadily improved.

At the risk of jinxing Harry's good health, I will note that he has been medically crisis-free for more than two years. Exuberantly running around and chasing tennis balls on all four legs, Harry seems to be doing great for an aging canine, now thirteen years old. Both Jesse and I are very glad we agreed to Harry's TPLO surgery. I even feel somewhat guilty that we did not bring him for surgery sooner.

So while I repeatedly referred to ailing Harry as "poor" in the sense that he was in a sorry state, his people parents were becoming "poor" in the literal financial meaning. While we unquestioningly paid each bill for the thorough medical attention and TLC, the accumulated medical expenses were astoundingly high. Although we were able to cover the bills, I seriously wonder how other dog owners handle such large financial debts for their ailing pets. Sadly, some animals may be reluctantly put to sleep for lack of funds to treat them medically.

When Harry began the first of his serious medical problems on the way to his $10,000 status, Tory was only four months old. That's when I decided to purchase medical insurance for puppy Tory—my first time obtaining health insurance for any of our dogs. The annual premium for Tory's VPI Pet Insurance for the first three years has been $240. Having paid a total of $720, we were reimbursed $650 for submitted claims—so far a fairly reasonable balance sheet, with a net cost of seventy dollars for peace of mind. We were billed a slightly higher premium of $273 for the fourth year of veterinary insurance. Assuming insurance costs will increase as Tory ages, it remains to be seen whether pet medical insurance will be cost effective over the course of Tory's lifetime. But, I am quite hopeful that we will not have to finance another $10,000 dog.

Chapter 14

In Care of...

There are inevitably times when pet-owning humans are not home and arrangements need to be made for substitute humans to manage the basic necessities of dog care. Although our Irish setters might come with us on various extended weekend camping trips from our home base in Sacaton, Arizona, we did not take them when our travels involved hotels or airplanes. But by living in a house with a fenced backyard within a small medical compound of personnel working on an Arizona Indian reservation, we could easily find neighbors for dog care in our absence. And, of course, we would reciprocate pet care when requested.

When we moved to Wellesley, Massachusetts, we were no longer so mobile. As a dedicated Harvard Medical orthopedic resident, Jesse enthusiastically worked long hours, overnights, and weekends. As a young mother and Boston University counseling psych doctoral student, I was simultaneously preoccupied. The rare occasions that we left our Wellesley home were family visits. When driving to the Jupiter clan in New York, we rarely took the dogs. And we never flew them with us to the Abrams family in Florida. But we lived in a small house with a fenced backyard next to a lovely family with three children and no pets. And fortunately, their teenage son Michael appreciated being hired for dog care in our absence.

When Liza joined our family in Weston, we did not have a fenced yard or neighborly pet sitting children. We still didn't travel very often, but there were some occasions that we would depart sans spaniel. At first I could prevail upon my brother David, who had just arrived in Boston to begin the Northeastern University MBA program about the same time we acquired Liza. I figured it was a trade-off, as David could get out of the city and do laundry at my house in exchange for pet sitting. But as David recalls, his well-intentioned pet sitting days were predominantly spent recuperating from partying city nights, crashing ignominiously on the school field near our house while puppy Liza frolicked untethered around him.

But when all of us, including David, were going to Florida for year-end holiday week, who would care for puppy Liza? Finding acceptable dog care was as worrisome as finding appropriate child care, especially during the busy holiday season. I asked a local friend with a sweet, aging golden retriever. She recommended a kennel in Randolph on the South Shore.

"That's pretty far away," I said. "How long does it take you to get there?"

"I don't have to go there at all," she said. "They pick up and deliver."

That sounded great to me: a kennel that came with a friend's recommendation as well as delivery service. I made my reservation immediately. Yet I still felt motherly pangs of guilt handing over our adorable six-month-old Liza to the kennel driver. She had never left our house since she came to live with us. There was no way that I could explain to my trusting puppy about her first boarding experience that she was not being sent away forever or that her separation from her home and family was temporary.

So I was thrilled to have Liza happily reunited with us on our return. But our poor puppy came home sick with very bad diarrhea. I wondered why. From the kennel food or germs being passed around? Or had poor Liza been emotionally distressed in unfamiliar surroundings? There really was no way to know. But fortunately she recovered with vet recommendations and family TLC.

With a summer trip planned to Cape Cod, I again reserved a place for Liza at the Randolph kennel. As she was picked up and taken away, I still felt guilty but hoped Liza realized in some canine understanding of prior experience that she would be coming home. And since we would be driving past Randolph on our return from Cape Cod, I arranged to pick Liza up directly from the kennel, which I had never seen before. And what I saw when we arrived was very disturbing. There was not one large kennel building or barn as I had imagined. Rather each dog was tied to its own outdoor doghouse. Perhaps that was fine for summer but seemed totally inadequate for a puppy in winter. Now I felt even more guilty about Liza's first boarding. I had never even inquired about the kennel accommodations, assuming they were fine on my friend's recommendation. That explained puppy Liza's returning home sick after her winter boarding. I would never use that kennel again.

That led me to in investigate other boarding kennels near us. I happily developed a long-term relationship with a family-run kennel in Sherborn that housed dogs in indoor facilities with outdoor runs. I knew it was a good place for Liza because she would cheerfully bound from our station wagon upon arrival. Although glancing back at me for reassurance, tail-wagging Liza always pranced excitedly to the barking greetings of other kennel residents behind the stockade fence. I likened her kennel stays to summer camp for dogs. Liza was a dog, after all, who did not require the cushy environment of our carpeted and comfortably furnished home for an enjoyable canine existence. The diversity of smells and sounds from the other kenneled companions likely provided an exciting change of environment for an only dog from a regularly scrubbed human household. Just the same, when we added Chelsea to our family, I was glad to board the two springers together within one kennel enclosure.

While the kennel scents may have been intoxicatingly aromatic to our springers, the pungent residual smell that clung to their fur was not sweet perfume to me. So when possible, I requested kennel dog bathing service before pickup to return home with sweet-smelling spaniels. I would still have to launder the smelly, dirty rugs I brought with them for comfort on the concrete kennel floor.

As Liza aged, however, she seemed less cheerful about her kennel stays. She was more hesitant than eager as we arrived for boarding. Then our friendly boarding kennel went up for sale as the family owners decided to move to a warmer climate. They hoped to sell the business so the kennel would be maintained, but there were no buyers who might come close to the offered price for the land, which was more valuable as residential housing lots. The kennel went out of business.

About the same time, I began to wonder whether staying at home would be a better option for Liza and Chelsea when their human family was away. We tried some in-house pet sitters who worked fairly well. By the time we moved to our second Weston home, Liza was thirteen and visibly aging. At the same time, Jesse and I were traveling much more. As an academic hand surgeon at the height of his career, Jesse was requested to lecture at medical society meetings and teaching hospitals around the country and the world. His career continued to dominate our lives. I had relinquished college teaching for more creative pursuits of freelance writing, which consequently allowed me the freedom to accompany Jesse on selected trips of my interest. Furthermore, Stacy and Ben were no longer living with us most of the time.

Vinny, our longtime reliable housecleaner, suggested that he could double as our pet sitter. That certainly appealed to me to have someone who was so familiar already with our family and pets (we had our cat then too). Well, the rest is history, as Vinny has been our go-to pet sitter for the past sixteen years.

But there is more to the "tail" as history always comes with a story, and there are a few more to tell. Vinny's dog sitting has involved lots more than just feedings and outings and exercise by tennis ball tossing. Numerous times I have left Vinny in charge with instructions to complete a course of veterinary-prescribed medication or feed a special diet. And when circumstances arose, he has gone way beyond the call of duty in our absence.

Starting with Liza, Vinny tended lovingly to our aging spaniel. Sitting down upon or arising from our tiled kitchen floor became a halting process for our elderly spaniel.

Liza eventually needed assistance to either descend or ascend three steps to depart or reenter our house. These were tasks that I performed as needed for a beloved family pet who had given our family much joy. I so much appreciated that Vinny treated her with the same familial understanding. And as I detailed in "Legacy to Liza," Vinny, in our absence, made the call to take Liza to the veterinary clinic when she seemed incapable of rousing from her dog bed. And that was where we returned to say our last good-byes to our extraordinary family dog.

Nine years later, Chelsea was our elderly canine with severe incontinence issues. Whether I was in residence or Vinny in charge, a pail and mop were always ready for action during Chelsea's downward spiral. As our longtime house cleaner, Vinny was quite used to washing our floor regularly anyway. I personally never washed our kitchen floor more than during this period of Chelsea's aging demise. Admittedly, Jesse and I had begun to wonder whether euthanasia should be considered.

In March, 2007, we were traveling in Australia where Jesse had meetings and Stacy was working on post-doctoral research in marine biology. Shortly after we had begun our trip, Vinny entered our house to find only Harry excited to greet him. There was no movement from Chelsea nesting on her usual dog bed. Assuming she was sleeping soundly, Vinny approached but instead found our senior spaniel in a lifeless state of permanent sleep. With our being so far away enjoying limited time with Stacy, Vinny kindly withheld the sad news to avoid spoiling our trip. When we were about to come home, he informed us that our once spunky second spaniel had expired peacefully—sad news but not shocking given Chelsea's recent aging deterioration. In our absence Vinny also made the judicious decision to remove Chelsea's body to our veterinary clinic for appropriate disposal. Once again, we so appreciated Vinny's levelheaded handling of this emotionally charged situation that was not exactly anticipated as part of the dog sitter job description.

To date, fortunately no more of our family spaniels have died on Vinny's watch, but that's not to say that his dog sitting days have been uneventful. As detailed in "Ten Thousand-Dollar Dog," Harry developed a life-threatening episode of hemorrhagic gastroenteritis entirely under Vinny's watch. While Jesse and I were away in Colorado, Vinny observed distressing symptoms of bloody vomitus and diarrhea, repeatedly cleaned the resulting effluences, consulted with us by phone, brought ailing Harry to emergency veterinary services in the middle of the night, and retrieved him with discharge orders for medication and feeding—all in our absence. A week later Jesse and I returned to find Harry in the same reasonably healthy state in which we left him, albeit with some remaining orders for post-hospitalization yet to be fulfilled. Again we owed quite a large debt of gratitude to Vinny.

And we have continued to appreciate Vinny's availability for dog sitting, even through Tory's trying puppy stage. It helps a lot that Vinny has found Tory just as endearing as Jesse and I have. He temporarily nicknamed her Mrs. Softie because her puppy fur was indeed so soft and downy. Now Vinny is impressed like us by Tory's stocky, muscular torso that propels her bursts of speed, especially to beat Harry to a tossed tennis ball. We are all similarly awed by her cute factor, particularly evident when Tory eagerly runs to greet our entering the house while dragging her favorite "blankie" in her mouth. Fortunately, Tory's sweetness counterbalanced the exasperating rock and furniture gnawing behaviors of her youth.

I am fairly certain that Harry and Tory prefer Jesse and I to be at home. We are their people parents, after all. But we can travel with confidence knowing full well that our canine family members are in very capable and caring substitute hands when Vinny is in charge.

Chapter 15

Groomed with a View

In our early years of dog ownership, I personally tended to most aspects of the grooming needs of our canines. The silky fur of setters and springers is not particularly high-maintenance but still benefits from the occasional thorough brushing to dislodge loose hairs, knots, dead skin, seasonal burrs, and other inadvertently attached detritus. As all our dogs have loved swimming, their playful water dunkings have often provided sufficient full body rinsing, albeit with residual *eau de* lake. But of course, there have always been periodic occasions when a soapy scrubbing is necessitated: when swimming is not an option over prolonged winter time periods, when normal canine body odor evolves from pleasantly salty to intolerably pungent, or when inopportune encounters with nasty environmental matter render our pets' presence offensive to the more delicate human sense of smell.

Spot cleaning and towel rubdowns are often sufficient. But when a full body shampooing is essential, I don old clothes and footwear, which will inevitably be sprayed by my shaking wet dogs. Even in chilly weather, outside hosing is preferable rather than interior tub submersion, which additionally necessitates post-operational bathroom disinfecting. My organizational process does not go without wary notice by my savvy springers who might try to avoid pre-bathing capture. So, I will proactively leash the dirty dog to deck railing to prevent escape from suspicions as well as the hosing and shampooing process. After towel drying sopping wet spaniels, I continue to deck leash them for further air drying. That prevents the freshly scrubbed subject from instinctually rolling wet fur on exterior ground, essentially negating my cumbersome grooming efforts.

On rare occasions I took our first springer Liza to a professional groomer for the full cleaning and deodorizing treatment complete with pooch pedicure. The poodle parlor requested early morning drop-off and late afternoon pickup, to which I compliantly adhered. However, I was admittedly uncomfortable with the amount of time Liza spent claustrophobically caged awaiting services on her day of beauty.

After kennel stays in our absence, I came to request pre-pickup spaniel shampooing to eliminate the distinctively odiferous and lingering kennel cologne, which would otherwise be clinging to their fur upon return. Bringing home a sweet-smelling springer was well worth the additional expense.

When we became a two-springer family, our canine grooming demands were thereby doubled. Soon after, I found a timely advertisement in our mailbox: Pawsible Solutions, a mobile pet grooming van that will come to your home by appointment. And from that point, almost twenty years ago began the start of an optimal relationship that continues to this day. Every few months I contact Karen Hayes to provide our spaniels with full beauty and deodorizing treatments in her mobile van, which is incidentally quite stationary in our driveway during service provision. Installed in the vehicle workstation, the dogs can view our house while efficiently receiving traditional English springer spaniel haircuts, with sleek head and torso embellished with graceful feathering on chest and legs. Interiors of long, floppy ears are wiped spotlessly clean, toenails are clipped, and paws and stubby springer tails are neatly trimmed. Overall fur may be seasonally shaved closer in summer or left longer in winter. Adjustments are made for young or aging dogs. Only once early on did Karen misunderstand my summer clipping instructions and removed all of Liza's flowing fur feathers. I was horrified to see the equivalent of a Marine buzz cut on our entire spaniel, our pretty pup who had never even had her fluffy fur clipped for the first half of her life. But just as I would rationalize when my own hairdresser has occasionally scissored my hair undesirably short, I recognized that the inadvertent removal of much old hair in favor of healthy new growth might be optimal in the long run.

Admittedly, the full beautification and grooming treatment is not as appreciated by any of our springers as much as by me. After prior experience in Karen's van, our springers are sometimes realistically reluctant to enter the confined space of hour-long grooming attention. But they always exit with cheerful exuberance, proudly prancing in their newly coiffed coats or just happy to be set free from the imposition of undesirably perceived ministrations.

Sadly, Harry is most fearful of the whole process. Karen tells me that he particularly hates having his hair blown dry. As with any knock on our door, Harry barks authoritatively at the visitor on the other side. But when the open door reveals Karen, Harry retreats to his dog bed, sadly shaking uncontrollably. We always send Harry for the first of two scheduled appointments so he will not be quaking at length in anticipation of his grooming nightmare. When all services are completed, Karen is Harry's friend again, and he willingly accepts her offered treats. And of course, he looks so handsome too.

In between scheduled appointments there is still plenty of grooming left to me. I still have to de-burr, segmentally clean, towel rub, or fully shampoo urgent conditions. Long-eared dogs are prone to waxy build up and resultant ear infections. Chelsea had the worst ears of all our dogs. She often required applications of ear medication and subsequent interior ear wipes. Neither Liza nor Harry was particularly prone to ear problems, but young Tory was diagnosed with her first ear infection at one and a half years.

"Does she go in the water much?" asked our vet.

"She loves to loves to jump in ponds and streams," I replied.

"Dampness is slow to dry in long-eared dogs," Dr. Kyrka explained. "And that contributes to ear infections." He recommended prophylactic eardrops, which I have been dripping weekly into both our water-loving spaniels' ears since I came to understand the likely origin of potential ear problems. Even Karen has remarked how clean she has been finding Harry's and Tory's ears of late.

While complete grooming includes ears, Karen does not clean dog teeth. That could be a serious occupational hazard. Since his youth Harry's teeth, according to Dr. Kyrka, were accumulating plaque more than most dogs. But the veterinary clinic does not attempt oral care either—that is, without anesthesia. So to avoid anesthesia for dental work, I brush

Harry's teeth weekly, with chicken-flavored toothpaste, as well as the teeth of his current resident springer companion.

None of the dogs particularly enjoys these grooming services. But it's a weekly project, ear and dental care, usually for two dogs. From years of persistent ear infections, Chelsea tolerated the drops with resignation. Harry, however, has always tried to twist his head and neck in futile avoidance of the dreaded drops. Chelsea was similarly belligerent about tooth brushing, to the occasional detriment of my fingers. Tory, I'm told by our vet, seems to be developing plaque early like Harry did, but fortunately both Harry and Tory acquiesce to their necessary dental care.

In addition to fighting plaque buildup, tooth brushing also counters nasty dog breath. Although admittedly, chicken-flavored toothpaste is not exactly the equivalent minty fresh.

Note: The chapter title comes from my eventual relationship with dog groomer Karen Hayes who arrives at our house in her mobile grooming van. Bathed, clipped, and blown dry in our driveway, the dogs are able to comfortingly view their home and yard throughout the grooming experience. Admittedly, I owe a nod of thanks to where I previously observed the expression "Groomed with a View," although in quite a different context. A sign announcing "Groomed with a View" is planted at the dizzying 12,000-foot height of the Telluride See Forever ski run, rightly announcing the spectacular overlook of scenic San Juan Mountains and stunning valleys. Telluride has become a second home to us, where our family vacations often, enjoying the beauty of all the Rocky Mountain seasons. My only regret is that we have never brought any of our dogs on vacation in Telluride as well.

Known for its scenic beauty, famous ski resort, and charming western ambiance, Telluride is also an extraordinarily dog-loving town. Every shop owner brings his dog to work. There is designated puppy parking in town, although many dogs are left leashed on dog-friendly sidewalks while owners dine or shop. Most hikers are accompanied by canines. The gondola between the town of Telluride and the elevated hillside Mountain Village has dog-designated cabins. In addition to lollipops for children, banks offer milk bones for accompanying canines. Water bowls are strategically placed for dog hydration. Telluride sports an AKC cacophony of canine breeds as well as much-adored mixed breeds. Even our apartment-style lodge has dog-designated units. Dogs are welcome throughout Telluride as long as owners respectfully clean up after them.

But our travel to Telluride, Colorado, from faraway Boston, typically involves commercial airplanes and connecting flights. And in all our many decades of dog ownership, we have never brought any of our pets on a plane. We have never owned a miniature pooch that could be easily carried and installed in the passenger compartment. Any of our dogs would need to be caged and flown as dog luggage. So despite our frequent travels, our occasional desire to bring dogs along with us, especially to Telluride, has been outweighed by the expense and potential complications of traveling with them.

Hopefully, however, some day we will be part of the plentiful pooch parade in Telluride, taking dogs on ambles through town, riding in gondola pet cabins, and happily hiking with them on well-trodden trails. Until then, our personal canine "groomed with a view" will be right in our Weston driveway.

Chapter 16

Gated Community

Sporty family dogs invariably present housekeeping challenges. When dogs share our home, there is so much more to clean and much quicker deterioration of furnishings and living space. Puppies chew furniture legs and baseboards and destroy pillows and throw blankets. Shed hair is ubiquitously distributed on floors, beds, and other dog- permitted furniture. Various body effluents, from saliva to other nastier drainages, stain carpets, bedding, and upholstery. Exterior dirt is almost unavoidable on house reentry. Mud adheres to all four paws and furry leg feathers. Seasonal detritus clings to various other body parts that have rolled around in the great outdoors. Doormats and dog towels rarely remove all the clinging dirty bits at the threshold.

In our earlier years of dog ownership, I was either more tolerant or more oblivious to dog dirt and destruction—probably some of both. Our Irish setters moved freely about our small, uncarpeted Indian reservation ranch house furnished with cast-off furnishings from my parents' household. Arizona Sonoran Desert dust infiltrated throughout anyway. No longer puppies, Lance and Brandy also had free rein in our cozy but newly carpeted and furnished Wellesley Cape-style home. I was too busy with infants growing into toddlers to stress over doggy damage.

Springer spaniel Liza was our children's first family dog in our freshly updated Weston home. Once reliably house-trained at about four months old, Liza was welcome throughout the house. By day Liza was often found comfortably curled up on the aging family room sectional couch, which had been demoted from living room centerpiece in our prior home. Fortunately, stains were not particularly visible on its burgundy-colored, sturdy velour cushions. By night Liza slept with Stacy or Ben, either delighted to bed down with their warm furry pal with little thought to sullied sheets. With admonishments and the occasional well-placed gate, I managed to prevent Liza from nesting on the new, more fragilely upholstered, coral-colored sectional in our redecorated Weston living room.

I also found another fairly innocuous aid to prevent pets from camping on a cherished seating area. The Tattle Tale™ is a small, vibration-sensitive, plastic-encased device that can be left on an untended couch. With the slightest amount of jostling, the trainer emits a brief, jolting auditory alarm, which typically deters the pet's potential leaping onto otherwise unprotected furniture. Tattle Tale successfully spared our expensive new sofa from springer destruction. Admittedly, however, our lightweight, sneaky cat often managed to gently snuggle at the far end of the couch without jostling the offensive trainer.

Free ranging throughout the neighborhood, Liza would randomly return home with varying amounts of attached outside dirt. And of course, spring mud season was the worst time for acquiring clinging filth. Sprints to and immersions in the nearby brook dissolved most of the offending deposits. On particularly mud-caked occasions, complete shampooing and hosing were necessary to make our wandering spaniel reasonably acceptable for house entry. But Liza was rarely pristine, and neither was our house. This was when our kids were growing through their school-age years. Our family dog was not the only culprit where cleanliness was concerned.

In our inevitably deteriorating abode, household wear-and-tear was not even under consideration as we brought springer puppy number two into our family. Two dogs, eight paws, double the dirt—an unavoidable fact of dog family life. And Chelsea contributed her own personal destruction. Busy with work and two high school-aged children, I did not vigilantly prevent Chelsea from climbing on my fairly new leather home-office couch. In keeping with our home's color palette, I had again chosen light coral. But I certainly had not taken potential dog damage into consideration in the selection of my lovely color-coordinated couch. Cushions can only be turned over once. When both sides were ruined, a washable throw blanket was the best solution to hide the dirt and damage. More carpet-staining dog accidents were noticeable too, even when puppy Chelsea was supposedly house-trained. Maybe aging Liza was becoming incontinent. Although I never caught either dog leaking or squatting, I was much too frequently applying the recommended solution of soapy water and clear vinegar to soak and neutralize the insidious yellow puddles.

After fourteen years of childrearing, dog rearing, house improvements, and renovations in our much-entrenched family home, I desired a change. So when Liza was thirteen and Chelsea was nine, and both Stacy and Ben were in college, Jesse and I built and moved to a brand new house nearby our old one. It came pristine! Every wall was painted linen white. There were no stains on carpeting or scratches on the hardwood floors.

So how to make that last? Our dogs could not have free rein within our new house. To keep our most fancy living space free from dog detritus and destruction, I decided to completely ban the canines from the foyer, the front staircase, and our combined living and dining room. That would also beneficially prevent our explosive springers from effusively greeting arriving front-door visitors. There are two interior openings to access those areas on our first floor and one at the top of the foyer stairs. But gating all never-permitted pet space would have been both aesthetically unappealing and physically cumbersome for us human occupants.

The solution I found was another inventive pet-deterrent device to place at each access point. The ScatMat is an electrically wired plastic mat. When stepped upon, the mat emits pulses similar to static electricity. Upon experiencing these harmless but surprising shocks, our spaniels immediately back up and discontinue further forward procession. All four of them have quickly learned to avoid entry into the banned areas—a training success. The banned areas have rarely been breached by our dogs. Of course, our cat quite rapidly learned to leap over the mats to avoid any shocking consequence. Most humans also learned to over-step the mat when barefoot. The shocks do not penetrate shoes.

The ScatMat worked great for never-ever dog admittance space, but there are still other rooms from which our dogs are only temporarily banned. When no person is home, we typically contain our canines in the least-destructible home area, the ceramic-tiled kitchen and breakfast area. The hard surface, however, is thoughtfully scattered with an assortment of dog beds for comfy resting. But there are plenty more times when the spaniels are prohibited from spreading residue of mud-caked paws on carpeted living space throughout the house.

Admittedly, a very common temporary deterrent is a door. But appreciating openness of free-flowing interior space, we do not have doors across all room entries. Furthermore, doors are not always the optimal deterrent. They are opaque barriers that are potentially pawed and ruinously scratched. So, alternatively, we have employed a variety of moveable and adjustable gates as well as assorted other low barriers to temporarily prevent our springers from selected room access. I wish we had no gates, but they are the compromise to decorating deterioration by active, furry, four-legged dirt magnets with chewing teeth and scratching nails.

In our new house, our not-so-new coral living room sectional became the comfortable family room crash couch for people, but not dogs. We were not concerned about Liza, who at thirteen years old had already lost her leap. But Chelsea might get some canny canine idea to climb and curl up, so I often strategically positioned the Tattle Tale. That definitely deterred Chelsea's camping on the couch—but not necessarily the cat. When I've wanted to bar the dogs completely from entering the family room, an expandable wooden gate has prevented their access. Although I still wasn't sure whom to blame for internal puddles, I certainly wanted to prevent surprise stains on the Oriental carpet.

When puppy Harry joined our family, he shredded the family room throw blanket and chewed buttons off the colorful African pillow covers—still more reasons to ban unattended access. Even when Harry outgrew his most destructive puppy stage, I was still protecting the sectional, and later the new replacement leather couch, from being taken for dog seating. I tried resuming Tattle Tale use, but Harry was just as sensitive to the alarm as the device was sensitive to vibration. The high-pitched emission upset Harry so much that I discontinued its use. Other human occupants hadn't complained, but they were relieved that the discomfiting Tattle Tale siren was temporarily retired.

Entry to our master bedroom is also adjacent to the breakfast area. Although the dogs sleep with us at night, they are not permitted to prance across our purple pile carpeting at will or bark and jump up at our large bay window upon viewing any passing person, car, or animal. The door can be closed. That's one barrier option. If the dogs are kept out of the bedroom with no people inside, the dogs are not particularly concerned. But if we are in the bedroom when the dogs are blocked out, paw scratching on a closed door is inevitable. A see-through gate, however, keeps dogs out while protecting the painted door. But it does not prevent puppy protest of their blockade by whining and barking to end their separation from favored people. Harry has found another way to request access through the gate. He swipes a bendable wall doorstop, attached just outside our bedroom door, announcing his entry request with a resounding twang—his own personal doorbell!

From our centrally located kitchen/breakfast area, I also access my small, tan-carpeted office with traditional door entry. As with our bedroom, it is optimal to ban dog access when necessary with yet another gate rather than close the door. When the dogs' feet are clean, they are welcome to join me as I run our household and communicate with the world from my personal command central. These days, when allowed access to my inner sanctum, both Harry and Tory prefer to be as close to me as they possibly can. If permitted, they either damply nuzzle my lap or camp directly under my feet. Squeezing under the desk and swivel office chair, they inadvertently tangle themselves among the snaking computer and electrical wiring. That's too much up close and personal, and potentially damaging to all the working office parts, human and hardware—so another barrier is in place. With a low, wooden plank, actually a recycled bookshelf, I physically ban the dogs from the back of my office. When clean, they can curl up in front of my built-in desk but not directly under my feet. "Low" works as I can easily high-step over the dog barrier. But through haste or weariness, I still occasionally trip the leaning bookshelf, which falls painfully on my heel. Big ouch!

The dogs may access our second floor by the back hall staircase. But since the entire upstairs living space is beige-carpeted, dirty dogs are disallowed. They can be blocked by barriers at either the bottom or top of the steps. Often we just lean a discarded window screen against the opening at the top of the stairs. That has typically been enough to deter our springers from entering a non-permitted space. Although the dogs will effortlessly spring over torso-height brambles and boulders outside, they are disinclined to knock over internal barriers that we have set. They particularly avoid contacting wooden gates, which are usually loosely leaning across openings rather than being firmly attached for easier human passage.

Having experienced the aversively ear-slapping alarm of gate crashing onto ceramic tile, the dogs quickly learned to cautiously keep their distance. Chelsea was the most gate-phobic, nervously giving wide berth to any potentially falling barrier.

There once was a recurrent mystery of pee puddles on the second floor carpeting and even the occasional disgusting number two surprises. How to explain that? Typically, house-trained dogs avoid eliminating inside their homes. But this was a new house. So perhaps our dogs only considered the first floor "home," given our house layout with most commonly used living spaces on the ground floor. Once again I wondered whether aging Alzheimer's-like Liza might be the sullying culprit.

But not long after moving to this house, arthritic Liza could no longer comfortably negotiate the fifteen hardwood steps to the second floor where she would have liked to accompany Jesse in his office. Then, I definitively knew that Liza could not be using the second floor as her bathroom. All signs pointed to Chelsea, whose house training, retrospectively, may never have been fully indoctrinated. Her puppyhood occurred during an exceedingly snowy, cold winter when Chelsea was reticent to leave the comfort of our home for the arctic-like environment. And I further noticed that Chelsea's pee puddles seemed to be located outside bathroom doors, especially when we had houseguests who were appropriately taking care of their own personal needs. That reminded me that the pee stains in our prior house were often located in the bedroom hall outside the family bathroom. My conclusion: Chelsea, smelling urine of strangers, was marking her territory like male dogs commonly do all over the great outdoors. But female

Chelsea seemed to have it all mixed up and was leaving her scented calling card indoors.

That settled it. Chelsea could no longer have free access to the second floor, not even visiting or sleeping with our adult children when they came home. She could hang out in Jesse's office only when Jesse was there. Other upstairs rooms were barred entirely. The barrier screen at the top of the back staircase was set in place most of the time.

Then another mystery occurred. When pet sitting, Vinny continued to notice pee puddles on the second floor, but the barrier did not appear to be disturbed. What to make of that? I certainly knew the "pisher" was not Liza, who could no longer climb the staircase. All signs pointed to Chelsea. But how did she bypass the barrier? I finally realized that the leaning window screen, while stretching across the upstairs access, was not Chelsea-proof. Unlike her fear of tumbling wooden gates on ceramic tile, Chelsea was not afraid to tap the light aluminum-framed window screen on the carpeted landing. Furthermore, she managed to nudge the screen away from the opening enough to squeeze her way past and also return the other way without actually knocking over the screen. Smart spaniel, but I did not appreciate her motivation. Once we understood what was actually happening, the barrier solution was easily improved by securing the screen across the opening with weightier furniture.

When Chelsea eventually passed on, and well-house-trained Harry was far past puppyhood, we could finally dispense with some of the barriers. Fortunately, Harry did not acquire Chelsea's bad habits, like interior territory marking or raiding open trash receptacles for used tissues and other discarded treasures. Of course, there was still the occasional gate to prevent muddy paw prints on plush carpeting or potential canine climbing on comfy couches, while I persisted in my attempts to forestall inevitable doggy deterioration of our abode.

Our minimally gated interior was a brief two-year hiatus between the time Chelsea died of old age and our acquisition of Vivacious puppy Victoria. The gates were resurrected and more so, especially during Tory's early house-training period. When our puppy was about six months old, I e-mailed her photo to my friend Sandy, a longtime Bernese mountain dog owner, who had recently acquired a tricolor English springer spaniel like Tory. Worried puppy mom Sandy's response: "What's that gate I see in the photo? How long are we going to need that?" Well, I suppose, that depends on how much dog dirt and damage is tolerated in one's home. And admittedly, I am more fastidious at this stage of my life. But I am reasonably realistic about the level of cleanliness we can achieve with two active dogs and one overactive husband, while fortunately factoring in a very reliable housecleaner.

Living predominantly on one floor, Tory was hesitant to negotiate a staircase. When I went into the basement, she watched cautiously from the top of the stairs but did not attempt to make a perilous descent. Nor did Tory try to ascend the staircase to the second floor, a veritable puppy Mt. Everest. I temporarily enjoyed the gateless access to our back staircase, but Jesse could not leave well enough alone. When I was not at home, Jesse joyously encouraged Tory to mount the steps to my last bastion of non-blocked interior space. There was no unlearning, and we returned to the selectively gated stairway access.

The staircase learning was not fully transferable, as Tory still continued to peer over the ominous basement steps without taking the plunge. As the basement door is usually closed, I did not worry about inadvertent canine access. So we eventually dragged reticent Tory down the stairs to demonstrate her latent ability to negotiate these stairs too. Now she cheerfully bounds up and down the basement stairs, shadowing me on my underground errands. And if I head to the second floor via the front staircase, where dogs are not permitted, I often find Tory has simultaneously bounded up the back staircase and is waiting patiently at the top to join me on the second floor.

Harry no longer climbs a staircase on a whim. He needs to perceive an important reason, like staying watchfully by Jesse's side to await the next communal outing, to laboriously mount fifteen continuous steps. At thirteen years old, Harry's ascent is slow and deliberate, like aged Liza and Chelsea before him. But in his youth, Harry did not even have Tory's timidity of stair climbing. He would typically follow me either up or down either permitted staircases without my paying much attention to him.

So one time I was in the basement for a few minutes, finished my underground chore, closed the doors between the finished and unfinished areas, and returned upstairs. After a short while, I noticed Chelsea outside but did not see young Harry. My dogs ask to come in and out of the house so many times a day that I can rarely remember if one or both of them are in or out. I ran throughout the house to look in all the rooms and also out through windows in every direction but still did not see or find Harry. I went outside to circle and call all around our property. No Harry. Back inside, I searched the house again. Maybe Harry had never left the basement, so I went downstairs, checked the finished area, and called through opened doors at both ends of the unfinished area. Still no sound or sight of Harry. So I pursued more looking around our property but to no avail. I loaded Chelsea in the Xterra and drove on nearby roads, calling for Harry from the car window, becoming more upset at his mysterious disappearance. I returned home with only one dog. Close to an hour had passed, and Harry was still missing. I worriedly called the Weston police to report Harry missing. Eventually I heard a faint bark. Where might that be coming from? I opened closets. No Harry. Exasperated, I went into the basement one more time, opened a door to the unfinished part, and standing forlornly in the dark was my sweet Harry. He must have followed me into the basement initially and was accidentally closed in when I first headed upstairs. But on my first cellar search, Harry did not acknowledge his presence by sound or movement. What a waste of an hour. But was I ever relieved that Harry was only lost in my house, not in the great outdoors.

So in my often futile attempts to foster cleanliness and to forestall eventual decor deterioration, I continue to selectively gate up our interior world. When Jesse takes Harry and Tory out for a run, I prophylactically gate the back hall entrance to the rest of our house. When the threesome returns with eight dirty paws and two tread-caked sneakers, they are forced to clear inspection in the temporary mudroom before further proceeding into our interior living space. Jesse's perception of what constitutes clean is much more lenient than mine. The younger and more active the dog, the more he/she pounds the ground, accumulating multilayers of dirt from paws to hocks. Young Harry used to be the dirt-dredging deliverer when Charming Chelsea was his senior. Now aging Harry's paws are lightly crusted while Tory typically returns a muddier mutt. Tory's ridiculous drinking habits only worsen the dirt factor. Easily overheated, thirsty Tory dunks most of her muzzle to lap water from the bowl, subsequently dribbling sloppily from her soaking snout. On water-dripped tiles, even slightly sullied feet stamp muddy paw prints throughout the kitchen.

I am forever toweling off dog paws, mopping paw prints, laundering dog towels, and readjusting gates. On the plus side: more energy expended, more calories burnt.

Gating Harry and Tory

Chapter 17

Bedtime Dilemma

Just when I thought I had put the Dogs in Bed chapter to bed, literally, there was an unpleasant new development. One January morning I disturbingly found a wet circle on the top sheet that was significantly larger than the damp areas I notice when either dog has been licking paws or other body parts in our bed. And this large wet spot had penetrated through the top sheet, duvet cover, comforter, bottom sheet, and padded mattress cover. I suspected inadvertent urination by twelve-and-a-half-year-old Harry because he was the old dog in the bed and the stain was pretty much where he had bedded down for the night. Admittedly, I didn't see it happen, so I hoped I was making the correct assumption about the perpetrator. Jesse, Tory, and I had also slept in our bed that night. I knew for sure that I was not the "pisher."

As I stripped everything off the bed, I was relieved that dampness had not penetrated the mattress, which would have been a lot more difficult to clean.

"We can't let Harry in our bed tonight," I insisted to Jesse after the pee discovery. "So don't move Harry's staircase bedside when you go to bed."

That wasn't so problematic for Jesse because Harry typically stayed in my office with me until I headed into the bedroom for the night. At my bedtime, I brought a familiar round dog cushion from the kitchen into the bedroom in hopes that Harry would find the dog bed to be a suitable alternative nighttime sleeping nest. But when I actually got into bed, Harry began unsettlingly circling our sleigh bed frame, seeking a way into the bed, and placing his two front paws on top of mattress and bedding. Although I didn't want to risk another nighttime accident, I felt very cruel keeping Harry out of our (his) night bed. Since I knew he had just been outside to pee, I acquiesced and moved the portable staircase, giving Harry his usual nighttime access to our bed and hoping the prior night's occurrence was just a random accident unlikely to be repeated.

And it was not repeated that night, nor for the next five nights, over which time I became rather complacent about the possibility of recurrence. But one week later, on a Friday morning, I upsettingly discovered a similarly large wet circle where Harry had bedded down for the night. And that night there had been only two other occupants, as Jesse was away on a business trip. Immediately stripping all the bedding, I thought about the prior night, which had been particularly nasty outside, wet and cold. Harry was probably not outside as long and as late as usual before bedtime. Jesse had not been home to offer Harry an oft-requested mid-night outing. And I had been noticing Harry's drinking longer at his water bowl recently.

What had we done with past aging dogs? I reminisced. Chelsea had developed incontinence issues in her old age, but we never had a "stairway to heaven" for her. She didn't always sleep all night long in our bed anyway. And when Chelsea was no longer able to leap into our taller queen-size bed, I did not encourage her to sleep with us, but rather kept a round dog cushion in our bedroom so she could bed down nightly on the carpeted floor nearby.

After two episodes of Harry's nighttime incontinence, I could not presume they were just random accidents. I called the veterinary clinic. Dr. Purbaugh could see Harry that morning. By the way, it's not all that simple to leave my house with only one dog. I have to plan it out like a military operation. I did not want Tory to go along with us because it's also very hard to remove only one dog from the SUV in the clinic parking lot and leave the other objectionable dog alone in the car. So I had to create a diversion in our house for Tory as I hurried Harry into the garage. I inserted a dog treat in a hard red rubber Kong© toy and tossed it to Tory, as she is usually delighted to busily chew on the Kong until the treat crumbles out. Quickly exiting the house, I could already hear Tory barking plaintively at our departure without her. As I got Harry into the car and pulled out of the garage, I worried about potential interior damage from Tory's frustration at being left home alone.

Dr. Purbaugh found nothing extraordinary about Harry by physical examination. So we would still have to await results of urine and blood sample evaluations for more conclusive findings. Tory was very happy to see us return, and our house was fortunately unabused.

With dogged determination, I vowed to be more firm at bedtime to avoid a third nonrandom overnight wetting with consequent damage to our extensive king-size bedding. Jesse was still away, so I made sure the dogs had an outing before I went to bed at about ten p.m. With decorative bedding removed, Tory hopped into bed as usual. But I did not proceed with the usual routine of moving Harry's staircase bedside, but rather placed a round dog bed alongside the people bed. Expecting Harry would beg to join us in bed, I intended not to acquiesce to his anticipated pleas. What I did not anticipate was Harry's own doggedly determined response. Shocking me, he spryly leapt up into the bed—something I had not seen him attempt since I had bought the portable staircase after his ACL operation more than two years ago. I had no idea that he could even do that anymore.

Harry certainly fulfilled the adage "Where there's a will, there's a way." But my "will" was to keep Harry out of my bed. So what "way" was I going to do that? How could I make Harry understand why he could not sleep in our bed? Unfortunately, no verbal explanation was going to satisfy our confused canine. Dragging Harry off my bed and banishing him from the bedroom, I partially closed the door and placed a gate across the entry to bar access from the kitchen. I've often placed a thirty-inch high, see-through gate when I wanted to prevent the dogs' free access to my bedroom. While the dogs would likely scratch and ruin a closed solid wooden door, they tended not to paw at the open-weave lattice gate. I also blocked physical access to the doorstop on the nearby wall, as Harry had recently been using it for a "doorbell" to announce his interest in entering the bedroom. When he hit the spring-like doorstop with his paw, it made a noisy twanging sound.

But this was a different situation compared to more commonly barred bedroom daytime access. I was banning Harry from his usual nighttime bedding place. And both Tory and I were on the bedroom side of the door, while Harry was alone on the kitchen side. Rather quickly, kitchen-banished Harry managed to maneuver his way past the less-than-securely-affixed gate and arrived in the bedroom quite proud of himself.

Giving Harry little time to celebrate, I dragged him out of the bedroom and back into the kitchen, put two portable gates across the bedroom entry, and firmly closed the solid wooden door. That left Harry furiously barking in the kitchen, as I tried to find some television program interesting enough to allow me to ignore Harry's loud laments. Tory remained soundly snuggled up next to me, surprisingly unbothered by Harry's unhappy howling.

Eleven thirty p.m. Although I had managed to fitfully doze off and on, I awakened to more abrasive barking. I sleepily got out of bed and let Harry and Tory outside to run around for a few minutes and take care of any personal needs. After calling the dogs back into the house, I let Tory slip into the bedroom while restraining Harry from the same access. I hoped Harry would tire out, but he did not calm down any better during the next ninety minutes. I channel-surfed over a range of late-night television programming to distract myself from his belligerent barking.

One a.m. As much as I did not want to leave the relative comfort of my bed again, I got up to offer unsettled Harry another outing. As Tory joined in, I tried to solve this dilemma with my sleep-deprived brain. When they returned inside, I banned both dogs from my bedroom, hoping Tory's company would soothe Harry. It might have been unfair to Tory, but their sleeping together on dog beds in the kitchen was not so unusual for them. That's where both dogs sleep whenever Vinny pet sits. Vinny does not invite our dogs into his bed at our house. But dogs are creatures of routine habits. They knew I was behind my bedroom door and it was the middle of the night. They were always in our bed under those two conditions. Why not now? Now I had two unhappy and confused canines. Tory kept whining by the bedroom door, while Harry kept barking by the sliding glass door. I was not getting any restful sleep.

Three a.m. I have to let them out again, I drowsily told myself, rousing shakily from bed. Upon my opening the bedroom door, Tory made an immediate beeline for the bed and rooted herself exactly where she intended to spend the rest of the night. I let Harry out and again pondered my next tactic. Given that it was already three a.m., how incontinent might Harry become before not-so-far-away morning? I surrendered, but not before I covered all the bedding with double layers of bathroom towels. I positioned the stairway to heaven because I did not want to encourage Harry's leaping and potentially tearing his other ACL. We were all in deep sleep within minutes.

Seven a.m. I awakened but could have easily put myself back to much-needed deep sleep. Harry was sound asleep nearby, and I fortunately didn't feel anything wet underneath him. But how long could he last? The thought bothered me too much to stay in bed. Tory was raring to go because it was time to retrieve the morning newspaper. I encouraged weary Harry out of the bed. Tory ran out to get the paper. They both got reward treats and headed outside to olfactorily discover the creatures that had passed the night on our property. Albeit sleep-deprived, we had completed a dry night. But what would I do the next night?

Realizing I could not take another nightmarish night of trying to banish beleaguered Harry from his rightful night bed, I made sure Harry had an outing as late as possible before I went to bed on Saturday night. Thickly covering the bedding with insurance towels, I peacefully allowed Harry his usual access by portable staircase. I planned to wake multiple times throughout the night (which I often do anyway) to send Harry outside for preventive peeing.

One thirty a.m. I reached under Harry. All was dry. I sent Harry out.

Three a.m. All was dry. I couldn't convince myself to rouse from the bed.

Five a.m. Phew, still dry. I roused and sent Harry out. We all went back to bed for another couple of hours. Another dry night.

With towels again spread atop the bedding Sunday night, the dogs and I went to "our" bed. At two a.m. I made myself exit the bed and wake the dogs to go out. It was still a dry night when we all got up at six a.m. for Tory to retrieve the newspaper. So maybe Harry only needs one middle-of-the-night outing, I thought.

Early Monday morning Dr. Purbaugh called with the lab report. As tests were generally in the normal range, Harry was likely developing some age-related changes and renal insufficiency characteristic of an older dog. No meds were indicated. I would have to stick with my behavioral tactics to prevent inadvertent bedtime puddles. When decorative bedding is removed for the night, lots of towels are piled on.

When Jesse came home from his business trip, he was assigned to monitoring mid-night outings for Harry. I still tend to let the dogs out once in the night, just in case Jesse doesn't. By the next morning, I usually find out that Jesse has let them out twice. Jesse and I seem to awaken at different intervals throughout the night.

For at least six months, we topped our usual bedding with strategically placed towels—just in case. But with no further puddling episodes, I eventually abandoned the towel-placing routine. I went out every night with the dogs to ensure I saw a pre-bedtime pee from each of them. And, all was dry for about another half-year. But one February morning, I discovered a dreaded puddle, soaking through sheets, comforter, and mattress pad. Argh! I reviewed my prior night's behavior on that chilling winter night. Yes, I had let the dogs out late. But, wearily reluctant to don cumbersome boots and outerwear, I had not accompanied them out of the house. Rather, I had watched from the kitchen to notice that both Harry and Tory had left the deck.

I presumed that the usual activities had occurred as they did under my surveillance every other night. But admittedly, I did not actually see their physical acts of urination. In retrospect, presuming was not optimal for pee puddle prevention—especially while continuing to indulgently allow our thirteen and one-half-year-old dog to sleep with us at night. So, I resumed towel padding and better night vigilance.

Yet by mid-March, aging Harry developed a new geriatric issue: inadvertent poop release. Harry appeared to have lost anal sphincter control. During daytime he contortedly attempted to elevate his arthritic body from his dog bed and poops popped out before he could rise and exit the house. Harry barked excitedly at workmen and poops appeared on the kitchen floor.

"That just started happening," I said apologetically to our renovations contractor. Swiftly removing the offensive plop, I was nevertheless quite embarrassed by Harry's bowel incontinence. Yet I was no stranger to geriatric canine incontinence. We had gone through the last year of Chelsea's old age with her peeing all over the kitchen floor, no matter how may times we took her outside for preventive pee purposes. A mop was always at the ready, and random kitchen pee puddles were gingerly avoided by tiptoe each morning.

Our veterinarian recommended changing Harry's diet to Hill's™ i/d canine food, a gastrointestinal friendly formula. So on the positive side, if one could call it that, the offending objects were generally firm, fibrous, minimally smelly, and relatively easy to clean up.

But I still had to make sure that Harry got out of the house on a timely basis, throughout the day and night to prevent inadvertent in-house poop surprises. And should I have banned Harry from our bed right there and then? Certainly. But did I do that? Insanely, no. Sympathetic to Harry's longtime attachment to our nighttime bed as well as anticipating agitated protest to bed banning, I still reluctantly allowed Harry to sleep in our bed that he considered to be his. But one morning Jesse found three little round poops on the carpet by our bed. Poops on kitchen tile are tolerable, but carpet mishaps are much more problematic. And to make matters worse, on another morning I found a small brown orb on top of our sheets. That grossed me out completely.

Meanwhile Harry had been developing another problematic habit. Instead of using the adjacent carpeted staircase for gentle bed exit, he had started jumping off the opposite side of the bed. I attributed this to Harry's attempt to avoid Tory, who had developed her own bad habit. With the excitement of morning arousal, Tory tended to pounce on Harry as he walked down the bed steps. I couldn't blame Harry for wanting to avoid an unwarranted and traumatic Tory attack. But I seriously worried that Harry might ruin his ACL repair or injure the other leg. If possible, I tried to shuttle Tory out of the bedroom and pull Harry toward the staircase before he leaped off the other side. But I was not always successful in orchestrating these mindful maneuvers in my groggy morning state.

One early morning close to the ignominious bed poop episode, Harry crashed very badly off the bed before I could grab him. He got up wobbly and limping, and I feared the worst. I e-mailed to Jesse at work that morning:

> "Harry is a mess, all wobbly and falling down
> he threw up trying to go outside
> he needs help getting up & down steps
> he can stand up and walk but not well
> that seemed to come from his having to jump off bed on my side, to avoid Tory
> I hope this is just temporary"

To complicate the situation, we were leaving for a long weekend trip later that day. Before leaving, I informed our pet sitter Vinny of Harry's unfortunate condition.

During the weekend Vinny sent us an e-mail update:

"Harry is very shaky & seems to be listing hard to his port side. He needs to be carried down stairs, but can come up by himself."

When we arrived home later that day, we did indeed find Harry "listing hard to port." Harry was not limping so I was no longer worried about another ACL injury. But I finally had no compunction about entirely banning Harry from our bed that night. I did not want to take the chance that he might further injure himself, in addition to the lingering concern for inadvertent poop release. But I was not optimistic about the process. I assumed that Harry would protest and that Jesse would be bothered by the commotion.

By the time I was ready to go to bed that night, and thus Harry too, Jesse and Tory were already asleep. Assuming that Harry would be more upset to be banned from our entire bedroom, I left the door open and placed a round dog cushion by our master bed. Of course, I did not move the three-step staircase into its usual nighttime position adjacent to our bed. I got into bed, steeling myself for Harry's confusion. And of course he was confused. He semi-circled the bed repeatedly, looking for his stairs and looking bewilderedly at me. I intentionally avoided eye contact. What Harry didn't do was of great relief to me. He did not vocalize his discontent, and he did not attempt to jump onto the bed. Harry was more than a year older than my prior attempt to ban bed access, at that time due to the pee puddle conundrum. That's when he had surprised me with his latent ability to jump on the bed. But this time there was no jumping or even placing front paws upon the bed. Harry no longer had the motor coordination or balance to attempt an entry leap. After about twenty minutes of pacing and circling, Harry finally gave up and retreated to his dog bed in the kitchen. So I finally could fall asleep too.

Having made it through the first night of Harry's not sleeping in our home bed with us, I called the veterinary clinic on Monday morning to address his imbalanced posture and cocked head. As soon as Dr. Purbaugh viewed Harry in the examining room, his diagnosis was as clear to the vet as it was a mystery to me.

"He has geriatric vestibular disease," Dr. Purbaugh pronounced. "There is no treatment for it, but it usually improves on its own." The diagnosis of an inner ear imbalance explained Harry's reticence to walk down steps. The nauseating effects of the vestibular disease additionally explained Harry's recent reluctance to eat and bouts of vomiting.

Tempting Harry to resume eating, I cooked chicken with noodles and hamburger with rice. As the vestibular disease subsided and his appetite increased, I weaned Harry back to his GI-friendly i/d diet. Although I could not help feeling sad and slightly guilty about Harry's bed prohibition, I nevertheless persisted in banning Harry from our bed for his sake and ours. Each night he was less confused about the absent staircase access to bed and meandered less time before settling down on a dog bed in our bedroom or kitchen.

While Harry's geriatric vestibular disease subsided, his geriatric sphincter control was no better. I could deal with removing the occasional excitement poop or inadvertent random plop from the floor, but never wanted to find one in my bed again. I am even embarrassed to admit the offensive event even happened at all, essentially due to both canine indulgence and presumption of anticipated difficulty to retrain Harry regarding his bedtime sleeping habits.

Tory, of course, is still snuggling up with us each night. And admittedly on the plus side, there is much less paw dirt and dog hair with only one-dog nights.

Chapter 18

All in the Family

Puppies come with an irresistible, innate cute factor. Big liquid eyes; smiley faces; short, stubby snouts; warm furry bodies; and a built-in desire to cuddle right up to you any time you will let them. That mostly explains why we overlook their practically incorrigible behavior with regard to youthful incontinence and their tendency to chew almost anything within mouth-capturing vicinity. And indeed, each of our six puppies captured our hearts.

Lance was our first foray into puppy parenthood. Brandy was his adorable little sister. Liza rounded out our household of two parents and two young children. Chelsea gave our teenagers the experience of raising a puppy. Harry filled our empty nest. And Tory filled our hearts with love at a time when we were sadly depleted.

Lance chewed off the edges of our LP record covers, tail-swiped an irreplaceable Hohokam bowl into pottery shards, insistently squeezed between us in our small conjugal bed, and uncontrollably ruined his handsome red coat by biting his incurably itchy skin. But we loved him.

Brandy ate a poisoned mouse, mindlessly followed wandering Lance on unfettered escapades, and carelessly trampled young Stacy's puzzles and plastic Fisher Price village people. But Brandy always gleefully greeted our house return with a favorite toy in mouth and a happy hind-side wiggle. Regularly accosted by Brandy's cheerfully exaggerated lip retraction, Jesse devised his own arrival exclamation. "Gimme those teeth," Jesse announced to Brandy upon daily re-acquaintance. Because he loved her.

Liza, given an English name to match her pedigree, became the darling of our family. Stacy and Ben met her as a puppy, and they all grew up together. They squabbled over where Liza would sleep at night, but ultimately it was Liza's decision. They loved her intensely and chased her playfully around our house and yard. Liza played the game and gave them extra reasons to chase. She intentionally stole their shoes, slippers, stuffed animals, sport balls, and hats off their heads, mischievously daring the owners to attempt recovery of their personal possessions. Liza saw the kids off to school in the morning and expectantly met their school bus upon return. Liza consoled them on their sick or lonely days, snuggling side by side on family room furniture. Of course, Liza was my dog and Jesse's too. But we particularly loved her for the way she loved our children and the way they loved her back.

Puppy Liza would ebulliently jump upon five-year-old Ben. Excitedly grabbing clothing with sharp puppy teeth, Liza unintentionally pierced through fabric and skin. "She's hurting me," Ben would angrily exclaim as he fended off his pouncing playmate.

Stacy, Ben and puppy Liza drawing by Stacy Jupiter

"She's just a puppy," I tried to explain. "She doesn't mean to hurt you. She's just wants to play."

Yet Ben insisted, "She knows she's hurting me." And admittedly most of Ben's summer shirts were hole-punched by puppy-tooth punctures. But no amount of my reasoning managed to convince Ben that Liza was playfully unconscious of the sharpness of her teeth. But this teaching moment was not fully lost. In developmental psychology classes, I offered Ben's viewpoint as an example of childhood egocentrism. As described by famed psychologist Jean Piaget, a young child is initially self-centered, only seeing his world from his own perspective, thus unable to put himself in "someone else's shoes," in this case "paws."

Conversely, Ben's developmental immaturity was sometimes bothersome to our otherwise sweet-tempered spaniel. Youthfully unpredictable, boyish Ben managed to aggravate an occasionally tuckered-out Liza. Wearily curled on the family room couch, Liza might utter a soft guttural growl to warn poking and prodding young Ben to back off. With some motherly intervention to separate immature boy and beleaguered dog, I swiftly acted to prevent the development of potentially unfortunate consequences for a pet-owning family.

Much of Liza's demanding puppyhood is a memory blur to me. But not to our cousin Claudia who was the recipient of a cassette tape in which I detailed the exhaustion of puppy rearing in our busy family life. As Claudia was living in Geneva, Switzerland, we periodically communicated by mailed tape recordings. In the 1980s, long-distance telephone calls to foreign countries were prohibitively expensive. According to Claudia, my unforgettable description of socializing an energetic puppy delayed her from obtaining her own family dog for several years. That was never my intention in recording the activities of the Jupiter family during the trying puppy stage of Liza's early life. The cassettes were just an inexpensive way to keep in touch.

What I particularly recall, however, about Liza's entire life was her easygoing affability with other dogs and awesome affection with all adults and children. Liza cheerfully greeted visitors to our home and made her own friends on independent neighborhood romps. When we announced, "Uncle David's here," Liza went flying down the steps to buoyantly greet his entrance. On our summer ferry trips between Woods Hole and Martha's Vineyard, Liza always sat patiently for other passengers' frequent pats and paw shakings. Young children especially gravitated to Liza's pretty appearance, smiley face, and friendly demeanor.

When nine-year-old Stacy was to attend a two-week session of YMCA overnight camp, we decided to make the drop-off a family weekend outing in New Hampshire. Liza being part of our family, we brought her too. After leaving Stacy happily installed at camp, we looked for nearby activities to entertain six-year-old Ben. We all rode the Conway Scenic Railroad as dogs were allowed on board too. But finding a motel that accepted dogs in the North Conway area was a challenge. After multiple negative responses along the main commercial strip, we eventually found accommodations at the Waterbed Motel—a rather bizarre place to me in more ways than one. Although immensely appreciative that Liza would be welcome, I observed the irony of a waterbed motel's permitting dogs whose claws might inadvertently puncture the bed. Fortunately, that didn't occur on our overnight stay. We also got the impression that the motel was more oriented toward trysting than family groups as they offered private sign-up times for their Jacuzzi spa.

While Liza was our breed of choice and first family dog, her breed popularity and visibility noticeably increased when the Bush family's English springer spaniel Millie became the first dog of the White House. From 1989 to 1993, I felt like we had a relative in the White House as Liza could well have been some distant cousin of Millie.

Our Liza was always eager to go for a jog or a walk. When Jesse went for exercise runs, Liza was his faithful jogging companion. Stacy trained for soccer season with Liza at her side. When I made brisk walking an exercise choice, Liza joyfully joined my neighborhood excursions. When Chelsea, another English moniker-ed spaniel, joined our family, Jesse jogged with two exuberant unleashed dogs. Exercise running has been mutually beneficial for my active husband and our similarly high-energy springers.

But as Liza aged, her hearing seriously diminished. Our calls literally fell upon deaf ears. When Liza ran ahead on our walks, I could not call her back to me. So to change directions or turn around, I enlisted Chelsea's help. "Get Liza," I instructed Chelsea. "Go turn her." And Chelsea did. Well, at least Chelsea ran ahead toward her older "sister," catching Liza's attention. With head turned, Liza could then see me waving her back toward me.

On outings when both Jesse and I took the two dogs, Chelsea watched out for both of us. Whether on summer hiking trails or winter cross-country, Jesse was typically ahead of me. After Chelsea ran forward to join Jesse, she usually backtracked to make sure I was still coming along. When we were once hiking a relatively steep ascent in New Hampshire, I lagged much further behind my fit and sure-footed husband. Inexplicably vigilant, Chelsea climbed the same trail several times more than the rest of us as she repeatedly returned to check my slower progress. I wished I could have ensured her that I would continue to follow without her checking on me. Chelsea's concern was endearing, but I wondered whether she was really worried about me or just wanted to keep tabs on the person with the car keys.

Eventually, I wasn't the only one lagging behind. As Liza further aged, she was the laggard. But she still wanted to go on any outing, and Jesse continued to take her running. One summer morning, Jesse took both Liza and Chelsea to a familiar run around our town's two-mile reservoir circuit path, a popular dog-walking locale.

"Watch out for Liza," I warned, additionally reminding Jesse that Liza had recently lost her dog tag, which had yet to be replaced. Jesse left without concern but returned in distress with only one dog.

"I lost Liza," he remorsefully admitted. "I thought she was following me, and then I couldn't find her."

"And she doesn't even have a dog tag on her," I bemoaned, worrying that our aging dog might be forever lost in the woods, stumble into traffic, or be taken by strangers.

We called in a missing dog report to animal control and quickly drove back to the reservoir. On foot we hurried in opposite directions in a frantic quest to find our missing spaniel. We inquired of other dog walkers whether they had seen her traveling alone. Promisingly, some had noticed a lone brown and white pooch and pointed where. Liza and I found each other first, with great relief for both of us. She looked as if she had been retracing her steps in a similarly anxious attempt to locate Jesse and

Chelsea. But then how was I to communicate our reunion to Jesse who was circling in the opposite direction? And, he was without today's obligatory cell phone appendage. With more pace than I ordinarily preferred to ambulate, I eventually caught sight of Jesse and relayed the good news.

Although Liza had been an only dog for nine years, we had brought Chelsea home for our people family to experience life with a puppy again. Nevertheless, we were all very conscious of giving Liza extra attention so she would not feel replaced or jealous. After surviving Chelsea's initially bothersome puppy stage, Liza warmed up quite favorably to her new little "sister." Admittedly, it took our five-year-old scaredy-cat a lot longer to adjust to the unwelcome presence of a prancing and pouncing puppy.

Meanwhile, the timing of Chelsea's joining our family in 1992 turned out to be more opportune than I had anticipated. And it was not just that her name was coincidentally the same as the daughter of the new United States president. Within ten months of Chelsea's becoming part of our family, Stacy went to college as expected. But rather unexpectedly, high school sophomore Ben also moved out to attend boarding school. Having gone to public schools, as did our daughter, Jesse and I were relatively unfamiliar with preparatory and boarding schools. But they are fairly common in New England, and some friends had already made private school choices for their children. We offered Ben, who was struggling among peers in the public school system, the opportunity to make a change. We anticipated enrollment in a local prep school, but Ben surprised us by broaching the boarding school option. We felt torn. Sending our son away to school seemed like relinquishing parental responsibilities. Yet we had been bumping heads over Ben's difficult teenage years. Perhaps his living outside our home in a structured environment might be preferable. And it was his request. We were not sending him away, although there certainly had been times I had wanted to banish him.

So by 1993 we had a premature empty nest. All of a sudden, after eighteen years of intensive parenting, my daily mothering duties virtually vanished. I was more upset than I ever would have imagined. For the month of September, I could hardly answer questions about my nest-flown children without breaking into tears. But our nest still contained two English springer spaniels and a cat. And they still needed me. And truthfully so did our children, in surprisingly many ways, without living constantly under the same roof.

Jesse was traveling more for work, attending professional meetings, teaching in short-term orthopedic courses, and being invited for guest lectureships. My work had evolved from psychology instructor to freelance journalist with more flexible work hours. While walking puppy Chelsea, I met a neighbor who offered in-home pet sitting services. With children out of the house and pet care covered, I was free to travel more too.

So in February 1994, I planned to accompany Jesse for several days to the annual meeting of the American Academy of Orthopaedic Surgery being held in New Orleans. Stacy was a Harvard freshman living on campus. Ben was boarding at the Pomfret School, an hour's drive away. A pet sitting neighbor was glad to care for our two dogs and one cat. Unlike Liza, however, young Chelsea could not yet be trusted to have the run of our house in our absence. Chelsea would have to be contained in her crate except for the sitter's visits and outings.

Despite attending college nearby, Stacy rarely came home during her freshman year except for designated school holidays. But, she had mentioned an idea about going home during the weekend that we would be in New Orleans. Some college friends might join her, which seemed fine with me. We did not discuss her plans much further.

"I'll let our pet sitter know you might be home," I said. "But call to confirm with him if it's definite so he won't be surprised to see people at our house."

Still in New Orleans as the weekend ended, I called Stacy back at her dorm and asked if she had indeed gone home.

"Yes," she replied tersely.

"And did any friends come home with you too?" I inquired, thinking about some of her new college girlfriends.

Another unembellished "yes."

"So how many came home with you?" I continued to ask, expecting a low number.

After an awkward pause, Stacy meekly answered, "Eleven."

"Eleven!" I repeated with much shock. This sounded a lot more like a party than a cozy overnight with friends in the suburbs. "So I can't imagine that all eleven were girls. Is that right?" I asked, finally catching on to the weekend scenario.

Stacy had hosted a coed overnight party at our house in our absence, without requesting any direct permission. I was stunned. But now it was a *fait accompli.*

"So which friends were with you?" I inquired.

Stacy related the names of both girl and guy friends, most of whom I had previously heard about during the course of her freshman year. Even after the fact, I was worried about a college party of minors at our house with no parental supervision, presuming there had likely been some alcoholic drinking and who knew what else. And what might I have said in advance if Stacy had actually told me what she was planning while we were away? I admonishingly voiced some of those concerns.

Trying to calm my post-party alarm, Stacy said, "But Mom, you don't get it. These are Harvard students. They even folded up all the sheets and blankets."

I guess the neatness of her smart friends was supposed to make me feel better about the surreptitious weekend activities at our absentee-parent house.

Becoming resigned to the completed scenario, I remarked, "Well, at least Chelsea got to be out of her crate and not confined so much."

Another awkward pause, which caused me to exclaim, "You mean you did not let her out of her crate? Why didn't you?"

"Because one of the guys, actually one I dated recently, is afraid of dogs," she admitted.

"You mean that tall guy that I met? And he's actually afraid of a little dog? That's ridiculous."

And thinking about how animal friendly we are in our family, I added, "So I can't imagine this is ever going to work out with the two of you." And it didn't.

Directly after graduating college in 1997, Stacy joined the Peace Corps. With long-term interests in marine science, she applied to the fisheries program. Her assignment was Gabon, a French-speaking country in west central Africa. Stacy expected to be away for two years. It was a tearful *au revoir* for me, but we hoped to visit Stacy in Africa at some point. But our beloved family dog Liza, at almost fourteen years old, was on an obvious downhill slide of aging deterioration. Stacy gave a long, meaningful good-bye hug to the special dog who had been part of our family through much of her lifetime. It was unlikely that Stacy would ever see Liza again. And she did not. Almost a year after Stacy left for Gabon, Liza succumbed to a combination of aging ailments, and we mercifully helped her pass.

Stacy's good-bye hug to Liza and Chelsea

Liza was the first of our dogs that I nursed through old age. Her elder care was demanding and time-consuming given her infirmities of mobility, cognition, vision, and hearing. But for all the joy Liza had given our family in her lifetime, I felt compelled to care for her with dignity as she declined. And I had no regrets for all the time and energy I spent attending to our Alzheimer's-like canine. However, after Liza's death, I was exhausted from elder canine care and in no hurry to find a new companion for Chelsea. I realistically recognized the anticipated exhaustion that new puppy care would undoubtedly entail.

More than a year later, we were vacationing on Martha's Vineyard, staying as we had many prior summers at the spaciously comfortable house lent to us by a generous friend. Sharing the generosity, Jesse and I enjoyed inviting family and friends to join us and appreciate our love of a unique New England island. In the summer of 1999, we were filled to capacity with family and friends, totaling eleven people and our one dog Chelsea. It was a bustling house full of love and friendship, but an undercurrent of worry. Several months earlier, Jesse's sister Vivian, in only her midforties, had been diagnosed with colon cancer. After surgery and radiation, her energy was low, and the prognosis was still uncertain. But we were all trying to make the best of Vivian's first trip to the Vineyard.

Noticing our English springer spaniel, the house gardener told us about a litter of the same breed at an island nursery called Heather Gardens. I was certainly curious but had been getting comfortably accustomed to a one-dog home with a mature canine and no exhausting demands of either puppy or elder care. But dog *aficionada* Vivian, owner of two beloved Rhodesian ridgebacks, urged me to visit the litter. So we made the pilgrimage to Heather Gardens. I had no illusions about my puppy willpower. Once viewed,

I expected I would be captivated. And indeed I was. The decision was not whether to acquire a puppy but which one.

The male I chose among Casey's litter of seven adorable springer spaniels was temporarily called "Stripe." Heather's family named him for the distinctive white stripe across his brown hindquarters. But to me our springer was immediately Harry, dubbed with an unmistakably English appellation.

Although seven-year-old Chelsea had been an only dog in our family for more than a year, she did not appear jealous of boisterous puppy Harry. Presumably, that was because Chelsea was not originally an only dog, having grown up as younger "sister" to Liza. And not that it made any difference to our dogs, but I discovered an actual bloodline connection between Chelsea and Harry. In reviewing their pedigreed lineage, I noticed that one set of Chelsea's grandparents were also the same breeding pair of spaniels who were one of Harry's eight sets of great-great grandparents. Technically, that made Chelsea great-great aunt to Harry, although that distant familial relationship did not deter playful hanky-panky between them—and they were both neutered anyway.

I was just as wild about our new fellow as the rest of the world was ecstatically wild about another British Harry, the widely famous Potter wizard. Our Harry's funny puppy behaviors made me smile every day. When tired and hot from overexertion, Harry cooled off by either splashing two front feet in the outside drinking bowl or flattening his furry torso on the kitchen tile with belly pressed to floor and all four legs splayed straight out from under him—both irresistibly adorable sights.

"I think you love him more than me," said our college student son, expressing some surprising jealousy faced with an unexpected resident male challenger to his mother's affections. But of course Ben also succumbed to Harry's playful charms, even bringing young Harry along on mellow local fishing excursions. While I recognized the opportunity for boy/dog bonding, I was admittedly worried about Ben's attentiveness to Harry's safety, or potential lack thereof. Fortunately, no harm came to our dog or usually not to any fish either.

Puppy Harry winning over Ben and Chelsea

I became even more enamored of Harry beyond his irresistible cute factor when he soon became our dutiful newspaper boy. With minimal instruction, Harry reliably collected our *Boston Globe* every morning from the end of our long downhill driveway. He brought the newspaper proudly into our house, nonchalantly accepting his rewards: a tasty dog treat and my enormously appreciative verbal praise. But I honestly think the praise would have been sufficient for Harry, who seemed to take great pride in his daily service.

Before long Jesse brought young Harry along with him on weekend runs with Chelsea. Jesse had been discovering many wooded trails throughout our suburban town and brought the dogs to trailblaze alongside him. The springers were always eager to hop in our SUV in anticipation of a wooded romp. Jesse would not think of running solo. He rolled the car windows down so our spaniels could eagerly thrust heads out of the vehicle and pant with excitement. That always reminds me of a Gary Larson *Far Side* cartoon. One space engineer says to another, "I told you dogs won't make good astronauts," while the drawing depicts a dog cluelessly hanging his head out of a space capsule window.

So after one local excursion, Jesse returned home to shockingly report that a similarly clueless Harry had sprung himself right out of our SUV as they were proceeding on a main Weston road. Thankfully, Harry was neither injured by his fall nor hit by another vehicle, and hopefully Jesse learned to limit the opening of back windows on future dog transports.

Having brought Harry home in August, I decided to keep our new puppy a secret from Stacy who would be returning from her two-year Peace Corps service in October. Admittedly, avoiding Harry in all my communications with Stacy was challenging, as a puppy in-house was such an all-encompassing part of my life. But I managed to keep the Harry secret—a mental effort well worth the finale to eventually see the delightful surprise on Stacy's face as adorable Harry keenly greeted her home arrival. We additionally welcomed Stacy home with a big family Thanksgiving celebration. Living up to his family nickname, Crazy Uncle

Jesse entertained our young nephews by squeezing into Harry's dog crate, prompting Jacob and Harley to do the same. Harry appeared more perplexed than entertained.

Caged in: Harley, Jacob, and Harry

On a visit to Vivian at their New York home, we also took Harry and Chelsea to visit their Rhodesian ridgeback "cousins." Jesse and I were pleased that young Harry was riding so peacefully in the back seat of our new Xterra SUV. That is, until we arrived and noticed that he had spent much of the three-hour trip chewing almost entirely through a seat belt strap. Meanwhile, after some initial territory issues, the disparately sized dogs were interactively friendly, especially the two young males, Harry and Rocky.

But sadly for Vivian there was no improvement. Her cancer had relentlessly metastasized, stubbornly unresponsive to various chemotherapy treatments. Weakened and medicated for pain, Viv spent much of her days on the family room couch. According to her husband Alan, their female ridgeback Vicky was Viv's constant and comforting companion, rarely leaving her side. And within a year after encouraging me to meet the Vineyard springer spaniel litter, Vivian prematurely lost her life in a brutal battle with an insidious foe. She left her despairing husband, two college-age sons, and two devoted Rhodesian ridgebacks. None of their lives were ever quite the same without her irreplaceable presence as wife and mother.

Back at our home, Harry developed into a macho alpha dog. He assertively barked his protective greeting when any stranger arrived at our house or property. But, I was not as sure that Harry was so vocal when none of his human family was around, as those who arrived in my absence had told me. So in anticipation of visitors, I often leashed Harry, restraining him while asserting my own alpha mom dominance until Harry's protective urges are quelled. But Ben and Stacy did not fall into Harry's stranger category. Each of them have only resided intermittently with us from the time Harry joined our family, but our savvy spaniel never barked at either of them when they returned home, even after long absences. Having been part of his puppyhood imprinting, Ben and Stacy were always family to Harry—another characteristic that I found so endearing.

In autumn 2003, my brother brought his Florida-residing family for a visit to experience the beauty of

New England fall. But with no animals in their home, their youngest child, six-year-old Sophie, arrived intensely fearful of dogs and began vocally avoiding ours. But coaxed to approach and pet mild-mannered Chelsea, Sophie gradually reversed her attitude from paralyzed to playful. The weather and foliage cooperated brilliantly for leaf peeping and apple picking. And thanks to Chelsea's sweet demeanor, Sophie returned home with a completely different attitude about dogs in general.

Dogs aren't so scary, discovers Sophie

Of note, my brother was also very fearful of dogs when he was young. Although we originally had a large standard poodle in the family of my youth, we no longer owned Gabrielle by the time my youngest sibling David was born.

Supposedly to cure three-year-old David of his fear of dogs, my parents brought collie puppy Andrew into our home. The cure worked, and we had our own friendly Lassie dog to complement our family.

Accustomed to pets in our Jupiter family home, our grown children eventually wanted their own pets. With a mobile worldwide career path in marine biology, Stacy opted for cats, whether in Peace Corps in Gabon, graduate school in Santa Cruz, California, or her professional position with Wildlife Conservation Society's Fiji project. Characteristically more independent, feline pets have been more suited to Stacy's lifestyle peppered with intermittent travels.

When living and working in Georgia, Ben and his girlfriend acquired an adorable golden retriever puppy that Ben named Loki. Recalling how raising our first puppy Lance provided worthy life lessons of love and responsibility, I hoped Ben would experience the same as a dog daddy.

Dog ownership is all about companionship and unconditional love. When my father died after a long period of illness, my mother sought to fill her lonely home with a canine companion. The last dog to live with my parents, their shih tzu Shanghai, had been gone at least ten years. In short order, however, an adopted one-year-old papillon became the center of my mother's world. Foxy Lady became the unrelenting reason to go out in her community, to walk the dog, or go to the dog park for additional exercise and pet playtime, providing owner interaction as well.

When both Ben's job and his romantic relationship fell apart, he decided to move and start anew in Colorado where he had happily gone to college. And he was taking Loki too. As parents, we worried about Ben's ability to care for his dog while in the midst of major life changes. On the other hand, we recognized how Loki would be a comfort to him. And fortunately Ben's friends in the Denver area were initially helpful with dog sitting when Ben was job hunting and subsequently took on a new position in medical sales.

When Jesse and I visited, we saw how our old burgundy velour couch, that had been Liza's crash pad of choice, had become the same for Loki. Amazingly, the sturdy sectional couch still existed, having provided seating in our three successive family homes and later moved with Ben through several states and living arrangements. Ben and Loki took us to their favorite local park for dog exercise. I was glad to see the bond between them as well as Ben's responsibility as a pet owner. Eventually, however, Ben realized that the demands of his work left Loki alone too much, and he sadly recognized that he had to give Loki up for adoption.

Meanwhile at our home, Harry had matured, and we had fallen into an easy autopilot stage of dog ownership where he was concerned. However, caring for aging Chelsea was becoming more demanding and time-consuming in her senior life stage, as had been the case with Liza before her. So I did not offer to take Loki, although I realized Ben would have liked us to be surrogate parents for the puppy he had raised. When animal-loving, well-intentioned young adults find their mobile lifestyle is not conducive to the demands of pet care, many pets eventually become wards of their parents. That happened, as well, in our extended family. When a student at New York University, cousin Claudia adopted a cute, friendly mutt from the North Shore Animal League shelter in

Port Washington, New York, but six months later Molly moved in with Claudia's parents on Long Island where she lived out the rest of her life. Similarly, when a student at Arizona State University, my future sister-in-law Tracy acquired an irresistible golden retriever puppy, but eventually very large, full-grown Blazer resided most of his life with Tracy's parents in Chicago. Years later Claudia also deposited with her understanding parents her Dalmatian. Ruby had lived with Claudia and her husband in Atlanta, Boston, and Baltimore but could not proceed with them to their international placements in Bangladesh and Geneva, Switzerland.

Had I taken in Stacy's cat Baja, as Stacy tentatively inquired upon moving from California to Australia for graduate research, I am sure that Ben would have pleaded for us to keep Loki as well. Even as a young adult, Ben seemed to keep a jealously competitive tally of comparative parental treatment in relation to his only sibling. Admittedly, I had mixed feelings but was disinclined to bring a third dog into our home. Sad but aware of his increasing inability to devote enough time to Loki care, Ben found a reputable, Denver area canine adoption center. Fortunately, as a handsome golden retriever, friendly and house-trained, Loki was very adoptable. Ben was assured that his young dog would quickly find another good home and new loving family.

During the next calendar year, Chelsea expired of old age. Like Liza before her, Chelsea lived a full springer life well into her fifteenth year. And once again, I had worn myself out with geriatric canine care during Chelsea's last life stage. But similarly I could not, in good conscience, prematurely euthanize a long-loved family dog because her care had become so cumbersome in the end.

Recuperating from elder canine care, I was perfectly content to maintain our household with one mature and rather self-sufficient springer. With more controllable work hours befitting a senior surgeon, Jesse developed a regular routine of jogging after work. And, of course, Harry was his zealous running mate, always greeting Jesse's arrival home with eager anticipation of their mutual off-campus excursion.

But admittedly Harry began to look decidedly more forlorn when we brought out luggage to pack. Through years of experience, Harry recognized that trip preparations announced that we would be leaving. Resigned to our impending absence, Harry would sit dejectedly nearby, belly lowered to the floor, front legs extended, and eyes woefully glancing at our advance activities that he was powerless to deter. Being home alone took on a new meaning without Chelsea.

But every so often, Harry can go too, on the infrequent occasions that we are driving somewhere that dogs are welcome. Such was the case on Memorial Day weekend 2007. Our widowed brother-in-law Alan had moved to a gentleman's farm in bucolic Sherman, Connecticut. Although Jesse was traveling for work in China, I planned to make the three-hour drive with Harry to attend the family barbecue on Saturday. Harry could run around the large property with his ridgeback cousins Rocky and new puppy Sammy. When Ben decided to come home that weekend for a friend's party, I explained my prior plans.

"Maybe I'll go too," said Ben, "if we can make it just a day trip."

That was fine with me, especially since we could share the driving. And I was particularly pleased that our physically distant son would have the fortuitous occasion to spend time with his cousins and our extended family. But Ben also had a secondary motive.

"So I can drive your car, right?" presumed Ben, referring to my relatively new luxury sport sedan.

"Not this trip," I informed Ben, deflating his eager anticipation of cruising in my Lexus sport sedan. "We're driving the Xterra because we're bringing Harry."

Although disappointed in the vehicle choice, Ben still decided to go and actually did all the driving. Nothing else was disappointing for us or Harry. The weather was uncharacteristically sunny and warm for the first weekend of New England summer. There was lots of room for dogs to run around, lots of food and fun for our people family, and lots of time *en route* for some heart-to-heart, mother-son conversation while Ben's personal mix of favorite tunes propelled our ride.

Never would we have predicted another death in our family just four months later—a shocking event that shook us to the core and from which we are still dealing with emotional repercussions.

Chapter 19

Why We Love Them

At the end of September, Ben died in his comfortable twenty-second-story apartment overlooking the stunning Rocky Mountain range from his downtown Denver location. At twenty-nine years of age, Ben overdosed on OxyContin®, a drug to which he had become secretly addicted. We brought him home to Massachusetts to be laid to rest. Among the myriad of emotions I was feeling, I even wondered how I would have felt to have adopted Loki. How strange would life have been to retain Ben's dog with Ben no longer in our lives?

Our house was a week of constant activity with live-in family overflowing the usually empty bedrooms. We were arranging for funeral plans and carrying them out amidst a continuous stream of visitors and deliveries of flowers and food. I was emotionally bereft, but the week was not a blur to me. I remember the surreal scenario much like watching our own personal *Big Chill*, replete with pathos as well as stress-relieving humor. Intentionally mimicking the movie scene, my late-rising but otherwise amazingly helpful brother David asked, "Am I the first to get up?"

As the intensity of the week wound down, I even found Harry wandering on his own in the living room where his entry had been forbidden throughout his eight years of residence in our home. Our lives had been turned upside down, and so had Harry's, at least for him temporarily.

When visits by friends and family dwindled, food was mostly depleted, and flowers had faded, we were just three: Jesse, Harry, and me. And Harry was the unwitting safety valve in our emotional pressure cooker of post-Ben existence, a living and loving buffer between two grieving adults individually negotiating the aftermath of family crisis so far out of the realm of our life and parenting expectations.

Not that either Jesse or I in any way considered Harry a substitute for our son, but having another living being with whom to share our love through the depths of this unfathomable tragedy was appreciably comforting. In repeatedly reviewing Ben's all-too-short life in my tormented mind, I even wondered whether I had been a better mother to our dogs than to our son. Or why didn't I have another child and fewer pets? But the dogs were not so problematic to raise, while Ben presented us with life complications for which we were quite ill-prepared to handle. Yet, there is no replacing a son and a thirty-year relationship of parental devotion and filial love.

We survived a year of horrible firsts without Ben. He would not be home for Thanksgiving or vacation with us in Telluride. Jesse and I would not hear from Ben on our birthdays, our anniversary, Mother's Day, or Father's Day. We would never call Ben again to wish him a happy New Year or greetings on his thirtieth birthday or any other future birthday.

Although awkwardly venturing out amidst emotional fragility, Jesse and I still continued to travel—and that left Harry home alone. So a year beyond Ben's mind-boggling death and almost two years post-Chelsea, the notion of getting a new puppy started growing on me. I had no expectations of filling the deep void of Ben's absence from our lives, but I began to feel up to the challenge of puppy rearing. And bringing a new furry bundle of love into our home seemed right at that time.

The presence of Tory in our lives simultaneously brought puppy-rearing challenges with the renewed influx of puppy love. Having planned ahead, I productively channeled the energetic demands of socializing our new charge into my self-imposed diet and fitness regime. Early Tory photos in our home show her contentedly nesting with Harry on his circular dog bed. But Harry's look and body language evidenced initial ambivalence, as noticed by my sister Carol, recipient of many e-mailed precious puppy poses.

So I have to share my dog bed too? Harry wonders

Physically withdrawing from the intrusive snuggler, Harry appeared perturbed by the uninvited invader of his personal space. But time-lapsed photography of two originally unrelated spaniels intertwined on a communal dog bed would eventually document the development of a mutually rewarding familial bonding. While Harry needed to be won over, attachment bonds between adorable puppy Tory and her people parents gelled rapidly. Right from the start, Tory captivated our hearts with her innate desire to be part of a pack, instinctively nuzzling into our family and our lives.

Two months into Tory rearing, we made another Memorial Day weekend visit to Alan's farm in western Connecticut, inspired by Stacy's return from Fiji to work with her Wildlife Conservation Society employers in New York. Somewhat sadly reminiscent of a similar family gathering two years prior, we were still eager to introduce Tory to Stacy and other family members, both human and canine. Unfortunately for Harry, he was recuperating from his first mouth wound surgery. So we opted to leave him home, driving in our new Honda CRV with only puppy Tory in the way back. This was young Tory's first long car trip since I had originally taken her to our home from her breeding family an hour's drive away. Our pup was surprisingly peaceful during the three-hour drive. But when we arrived and went to let her out, we discovered that Tory had vomited on the blanketed padding we had provided. We felt so bad for our poor carsick puppy, but she fortunately revived rapidly upon vehicle exit. We had another fine day down on the farm, ushering in the onset of summer among family and fond canines, despite lingering bittersweet memories of the past holiday barbecue that had included Ben.

Tory developed a puppy habit that she continues to this day. Anytime she is aware that I have gone into our lavatory off the kitchen, which is almost always, she comes running to be with me and score some one-to-one "quality" time with her indisposed mommy—very reminiscent of the lack of privacy I experienced when our human toddlers followed me everywhere in the house, including the bathroom. So now I multi-task petting Tory rather than catching up on any of the magazines strategically placed near the commode. As soon as I reach for toilet paper, Tory takes a cue, turns, and exits the little room—very funny and sweet too.

Meanwhile Jesse and Tory have developed a very special daddy-doggy relationship. As soon as Tory was reliable enough, Jesse allowed her to join his off-property excursions with Harry. Tory's anticipatory exhilaration to run with the pack youthfully equals or perhaps surpasses Harry's similarly eager emotions. Upon hearing the recognizable mechanical humming of garage door opening, vigilant Tory announces Jesse's arrival with spirited barking and exuberant sprinting to greet her favorite knight upon entry. Yet admittedly, Tory is still fooled by the similar mechanical sound of the washing machine spin cycle, frequently setting off an irritating bout of anticipatory but erroneous announcement barks. Additionally disturbing to me, the painted wooden door trim has been repeatedly gouged by uncontrollably excited paws. But the downside of Tory's excitement is far outweighed by the unmitigated daily happiness with which Jesse is ecstatically greeted upon return home.

While commuting after work, Jesse just as eagerly anticipates getting home to play with the "kids." My welcome-back acknowledgement and perfunctory cheek peck for Jesse are emotionally bland compared to Tory's exaggerated butt wiggle, blankie lovingly grasped in mouth, and oft times reflex excitement pee dribble. And of course, Harry still contributes to the overall welcome of quotidian canine cacophony.

The love does not stop at the door. While Jesse changes into his play clothes behind gated bedroom door, vociferous Tory impatiently whines staccato vocalizations of increasing decibels until they're finally off. Then the cheerful threesome energetically bursts out of the house to run and shag tennis balls.

The dogs are always part of Jesse's weekend routine of early morning runs. They all hop in the SUV to head to a woodsy town trail where there are multiple route choices for exercise and exploratory sniffing. The ground is soft on Jesse's knees, and the trails are relatively isolated. On Sunday there is usually an extra stop. Post-exercise the dogs remain in the car while Jesse visits the cemetery located nearby. At Ben's gravesite, Jesse takes the time to reflect on Ben's life, recites the Jewish memorial prayer of *kaddish* for Ben, and leaves behind a small rock on the monument to chronicle his visit. Five years after Ben's death, the top of the grave marker is piled with small stones, most placed by Jesse on his Sunday visits. The intense grief is slow to diminish but is temporarily mitigated by returning to a car full of unconditional canine adoration.

Jesse has a workday morning routine with the dogs too, all going on while I am still fairly sound asleep in bed. By five a.m. the dogs are let out for early morning necessities. But more importantly for Tory, she eagerly bounds through the garage to claim the newspaper and return it to Jesse indoors for her treat. There are still more treats for both dogs while Jesse eats breakfast and makes his work lunch. Each dog is the appreciative beneficiary of one egg yolk. Cholesterol-conscious Jesse eats only the whites of hard-boiled eggs that he has personally prepared in advance. Hopefully, the daily high-density cholesterol in the protein orb consumed by each dog is counteracted by their high-energy lifestyle.

The mainstay of Jesse's work lunch is his self-made, mustard inundated turkey sandwich. During its composition, Jesse always tosses a half slice of deli turkey to each dog. Personally, I think that he's wasting expensive turkey breast lunchmeat on indiscriminate canine palates, but I am not about to interfere with Jesse's special bonding routine with our precious pets.

Once Jesse departs for work, the dogs return to bed with me, Tory typically snuggling more on my side of the bed. Knowing the dogs have been outside already, I can peacefully remain in bed for a couple more hours till my preferred arousal time. The extra sleep I am afforded predominantly compensates for the excess dirt that often arrives in bed on eight early-morning paws. Meanwhile, I occasionally find one leftover egg yolk, expressly assigned to Harry, in the refrigerator if our elder springer opted to sleep in with me earlier that morning.

We have settled into a nighttime routine as well. Of late Jesse is typically first to bed down for the night. And he is always accompanied by cuddling canine companion Tory. Cozily snuggling, they wind down from their active day in tandem, often engaging in a silly game of bedtime handshakes and footsies. Loyal Harry keeps me company in my office until my later bedtime, only mounting our king-size bed when I prepare for sleep. Lately, as I perform my final bedtime tidying, Harry follows my every move—like a dog! From office to kitchen to bathroom to bedroom and any other combination of nighttime maneuvers, he awaits my final ascendance to our communal bed.

Harry makes himself comfortable at the foot end of our bed, although not necessarily so comfortable for my outstretched legs. An equal opportunity snuggler, Tory usually greets my bed entry by cozying up to me whether I want her intrusion or not. My desire for a reasonable amount of mattress space is usually won over by the endearing, warm, furry being who begs to be snuggled and stroked. There may not be a lot of space in our two-dog nights, but there is always a lot of love in our bed.

Although imbued with lovable qualities, no dog of ours has been perfect. All have problematic habits that have been difficult to deter. Lance gnawed his skin. Brandy mindlessly followed Lance on his far-flung escapades. Liza stole hats off children's heads. Chelsea squabbled jealously over food. Alpha dog Harry barks challengingly at visitors. Tory greets loved ones with an excited pee dribble.

But how have we loved them? Let me count the ways: our dogs are always happy to see us, they always want to be near us, and they always want to go with us. They keep us fit, and they keep us young. They make us smile, they make us laugh, and they lift our hearts.

Despite the work, energy, expense, mess, and bouts of aggravation of pet ownership and socialization, our darling dogs have been the loving, furry glue that has bound our family through the ups and downs of marital and family life.

Chapter 20

Tail-ending Verse

In our marriage and family of forty years plus
We've owned six sporty dogs that have lived with us

Our very first pup was an adorable Irish setter
Young & married with a dog, what could be better?
Actually Lance's behavior, he was wild with energy
Jesse busy doctoring, so Lance's training fell to me

We went to obedience classes, and practiced each day
Lance amazingly learned how to come, heel, and stay
Our handsome red setter joined our Arizona explorations
A great canine companion on camping vacations

If one dog was fun, then how would two be?
It didn't take that long for us to see
I looked for a "sister" of the same sporty breed
And brought cute Brandy home to follow Lance's lead

Our two rusty red canines shaped our active lifestyle
They loved jumping in our Jeep for a journey or a mile
They were our first children, they slept in our bed
They added excitement to the life that we led

When children Stacy and Ben were seven and five
We added a new family dog to our busy hive
The English springer spaniel was the breed I'd been eyeing
And little Liza was the selection from the litter we were buying

We had learned that Irish setters weren't known for their brain
But our new springer spaniel was quick and easy to train
She was loving and bright and adored by us all
She had an independent life but always came to our call

Liza watched over her brood like a much-concerned nanny
Her awareness of the school bus was almost uncanny
She'd make her choice on any given night
In which kid's bed she slept when they turned off the light

For nine years dear Liza was top dog in our house
But not the only pet, as we had a cat and Stacy's mouse
But the idea of two dogs was discussed by Ben and me
That's how we ended up bringing home Chelsea

Another springer spaniel of Liza's coloration
Chelsea cheered us with her sweetness and adulation
We were careful to give Liza lots of extra affection
So she wouldn't be jealous or feel any rejection

Once again we became a two-dog family
I even grudgingly let Chelsea sleep with me
But I didn't let her roam, like streetwise Liza in the 'hood
If she was hit by a vehicle, that wouldn't be good

So Chelsea was our first to be invisibly fenced
On our sufficiently large properties, and hence
Dogs could go outside for relief and exercise
Without being restrained or watched by our eyes

Liza lived a long dog's life, a dear companion to us all
She was almost fifteen when she took her final fall
That left Chelsea an only dog, where she'd always been number two
After a while, I began wondering what I ought to do

On a Martha's Vineyard vacation the answer came to me
A litter of springer spaniels for sale we learned fortuitously
That's how Wild about Harry came home to live with us
Although leaving his cozy litter he understandably made a fuss

Not an only dog to start, Chelsea showed no jealousy
She seemed even more relaxed with new pal Harry
Another smart springer, Harry adapted to our house
And filled in the gaps, as our grown kids had moved out

Raising a darling puppy is not all fun and games
They are adorable and cuddly but must be socialized to tame
It takes a lot of vigilance regarding chewing and peeing
They get into trouble when I'm not always seeing

The Puppy Diet

The first year or two are challenging the most
But finally dogs are easy and we can just coast
Until senior canine life incapacitates them some
And I have to return to a busier dog mom

As Harry grew into a stellar family pet
More and more, aging Chelsea would need to see the vet
Chelsea finally expired at a ripe old dog age
But I was in no hurry to replace her at that stage

I was worn out and tired from elder dog care
And needed time to recuperate, it was only fair
Though Harry was missing his pack of two
And once again, I had to decide what to do

If elder care was exhausting, it didn't even compare
To raising a puppy, as I had our fair share
In recognition of the energy I expected to expend
I planned a diet around the puppy that I would tend

Adorable Tory filled our hearts with love and joy
She was a cute little girl to join our handsome boy
But it took constant exertion to socialize our pup
I rarely sat down, I was always up

At the same time I was careful to watch what I ate
And happy to find that I was losing some weight
The puppy diet became the perfect combination
Of overexertion and healthy food rations

So now I have reached the tail end of my story
Of Lance, Brandy, Liza, Chelsea, Harry, and Tory

Liza and Chelsea at Martha's Vineyard
painted by Stacy Jupiter

Epilogue

On June 25, 2013, Harry turned 14. I proudly posted a birthday tribute on The Puppy Diet Facebook page that I had created in conjunction with this book. Announcing that we were still Wild about Harry, I included a more recent photo of an elder but still handsome Harry as well as two adorable puppy pics. One photo shows little Harry amusingly standing with his two front paws in his water bowl, attempting to further cool himself after drinking. The other photo is of exhausted puppy Harry preciously flattened on the kitchen tile floor with all four legs splayed out.

I was well aware that this might be the one and only time I would post a birthday announcement for Harry like this. Neither Liza nor Chelsea had lived until their fifteenth birthdays. And although his spirit was still quite willing for exercise walks and runs, Harry was clearly in the geriatric stage of his canine existence. In the routine process of lying down or rousing up, he became increasingly more awkward and rigid. He slept deeper and lengthier on his dog bed during the day. Having trouble going down stairs, Harry developed a preferred way to descend from ground floor of our house to outside lawn level, four steps below. He would only take one step down, and then tended to leap from the third step up, onto worryingly-hard concrete garage floor or bluestone patio landings. Having frighteningly seen Harry's uncontrollably sliding down two-thirds of a wooden staircase from our second story and crashing onto unforgiving ceramic tile floor, I began blocking staircase access and was especially relieved when he gave up walking up or down indoor stairs all together.

Even less interested in his dog food than usual, Harry was losing weight. Tempting him to eat more, I was adding at both breakfast and dinner spoonfuls of canned wet Hill's™ i/d dog food to the i/d kibble, vet-recommended for a more gentle gastrointestinal diet. Although Harry's weight kept slipping and physique was more bony, he still ate enough to poop, particularly noticeable because of declining anal sphincter control. Poops would occasionally pop right out of Harry, sometimes from excitement, other times from inability to rise up and get himself outside in time, or even quite randomly. I was spending more time outside with Harry, to ensure he took care of business. If left on his own, Harry might not even descend from the deck or might return prematurely from lawn level with nothing being done. Jesse had to stop transporting the dogs in our SUV for exercise due to Harry's excitement poop dropping in the way back, made significantly worse by two dogs stomping on uncontrollably expelled deposits.

On the positive side, Harry had recovered from an acute crisis of geriatric vestibular disease. A recent batch of blood tests was fairly normal for a dog of his age. Prescribed Rimadyl for arthritis and stiffness, Harry's movement and activity level appeared noticeably improved. But admittedly, when buying Harry's preventive heartworm and tick medications, I pondered how many monthly doses to purchase in advance.

So as we left Harry and Tory in Vinny's experienced pet sitting hands on July 2, I had only a few special instructions regarding elder Harry care. Encourage Harry to eat his meals. Administer the chewable Rimadyl pill twice daily meal times. Help Harry down steps to go outside the house. And watch out for random poops in the house that may have inadvertently popped out of Harry.

An unusual e-mail request from Vinny on the evening of July 3rd to call him was ominously worrisome. Harry, Vinny told me, was having a particularly difficult time standing himself up on the tiled kitchen floor. And he was having repeated accidents on the floor and dog beds because of his inability to get up to take care of necessities in a timely manner. We recognized that our local veterinary clinic would be closed for the holiday.

Because Harry was able to get some footing to stand himself on the lawn, Vinny kept him outside much of July 4th, in a shaded area with water nearby, occasionally hosing him down for both cooling and cleanliness purposes. By nighttime, exhausted Harry crashed on his dog bed inside. But hearing Harry noisily awaken overnight, Vinny found him thrashing around on the floor, unable to raise himself. Even taken outdoors, Harry could not stand himself up. Vinny made the decision to take our distressed dog to emergency veterinary services at four a.m. He then sent the following e-mail to Jesse and me:

> "I told them to just make Harry comfortable until they can reach you as opposed to the long list of diagnostic procedures they could do. He was really

flailing away, trying to stand, but could no longer remain upright even with my help. You can call them as soon as you see this."

About six a.m. Colorado mountain time (eight a.m. at home), early-rising Jesse read Vinny's e-mail, woke me to read the bad news, and left for his meeting. Bleary-eyed and non-caffeinated, I called the veterinary hospital and spoke to the vet on call. Harry had been admitted with a fever of 105 degrees and heart rate of 200, but with administration of IV fluids and pain meds he was in a more stable condition although still not able to stand on his own. The collapsing of his hind legs was likely a neurological problem although identifying conclusive causation would require further diagnostic procedures. This was on a Friday morning. We were due home late Sunday afternoon. Several options were diplomatically presented: a most aggressive, potentially revealing, and expensive diagnostic protocol including MRI; moderately expensive diagnostic X-rays and blood work; palliative care until we returned home; or the ultimate goodbye.

And what if we opted for MRI and received conclusive findings, but the corrective treatment was major surgery and lengthy recuperation? Would we even want to submit our geriatric canine to that medical path? Not likely. I toyed with the idea of doing nothing. But the vet noticed Harry was improving slightly, able to walk with sling assistance, and thought we might uncover a treatable problem with x-rays and blood tests. Jesse and I agreed to that.

The radiographic findings were read as "non-remarkable." Blood tests evidenced some elevated liver functions, a possible side- effect from prescription Rimadyl but not conclusive. Meanwhile, Harry was reluctant to eat. And unable to stand and ambulate on his own, despite being periodically moved by clinic staff, he was developing bed sores. Signs still pointed to neurological deterioration.

Although I would have liked to personally say good-bye to Harry, as we had done with Liza before she was mercifully put to sleep, I did not want him to be suffering longer in our absence.

"It sounds like it's time to say good-bye," I said to the vet on call, as I choked back tears. She did not argue with me, and seemed supportive of the conclusion that appeared inevitable.

"But I'll just talk to my husband first, and get back to you," I told her.

I was relieved that Jesse answered his cell phone, even though he was in the midst of his meeting. Hearing the current status of Harry's condition and tests, Jesse agreed with the decision to put our ailing and failing guy to sleep that day rather than wait until our return for a final and likely tearful good-bye. Recognizing I was indeed becoming increasingly weepy, I asked Jesse to make the call to the vet clinic to authorize Harry's euthanasia. I was rationally accepting of this endpoint but was surprisingly emotional about the seemingly abrupt conclusion to our life with Harry.

As with Liza and Chelsea before him, we did not choose to do anything special with Harry's remains. Harry would be incinerated in a group animal cremation and all the ashes would be spread in a pet cemetery. That was fine with me. But I know his memory will live on in our hearts and in the myriad of Harry photos from absolutely adorable puppyhood through venerable companion to me, Jesse and Tory.

And speaking of Tory, I was immediately concerned for her reaction to Harry's absence and existing as an only dog at home. According to Vinny, Tory seemed more perplexed when Harry was debilitated in the house. But after Harry was hospitalized, Vinny e-mailed that "Tory seems to be her same old self. I don't see any changes. She fetches, eats well, and hides behind her blanket."

But naturally I had to see for myself, and kept a close eye on her upon my return. Tory did indeed seem subdued at first, but the weather may have been contributory. It had been hot, gray, humid and rainy—just the kind of weather that typically makes our dogs hunker down rather than spring spiritedly around our house and yard. So I took Tory with me on short errands, if not too hot to leave her briefly in the car.

The house did seem rather strange without Harry in it. I did not have to coax a dog to eat and administer medication. No dog needed help going outside or down a few steps to the yard. I did not have to accompany a dog multiple times during the day and night to prevent inadvertent in-house pooping. There were no surprise poops to clean up inside. There were only four paws to clean when Jesse came back from running with one dog. We no longer had Harry's incessant requests to go out and come back in moments later. I did not have to forewarn visitors about Harry's protective and proprietary attitude.

But of course, we also no longer had Harry, our top dog, our first newspaper delivery dog, Jesse's running companion, my protector, and Tory's big brother. Goodbye sweet Harry. We are missing you.

Appendix

Puppy Diet Foods

Beryl's personal food choices, hints, and suggestions

- Eat only foods that taste good to you.
- Use fat-free milk. Try Over the Moon® from Garelick Farms, which doesn't even taste fat-free as extra amounts of calcium and protein really make it "rich and creamy," as they advertise, without adding calories.
- Do not bother eating fat-free foods that are substitutes for foods that are largely based on fat, like fat-free cheese. How could that taste good? Eat low-fat dairy products when they are tasteful substitutes for the original foods, like ricotta, mozzarella, or cottage cheese. Try Hellmann's® light mayonnaise. Use healthy fats like olive and canola oils. Lightly spray on *I can't believe it's not Butter!*® when pan frying to minimize fat used.
- Eat lots of salad at lunch and dinner. Use low-fat salad dressing, lightly applied. I absolutely adore Maple Grove Farms of Vermont® sesame ginger dressing at only forty-five calories per two tablespoons. Other favorite low-calorie dressings include Newman's Own® Lite Balsamic Vinaigrette and Lite Honey Mustard and Ken's Steak House® Lite Balsamic Vinaigrette. Wishbone's spray-on Salad Spritzers®

help minimize the amount of dressing applied. Make salads colorful, tasty, and interesting with a variety of veggies. Add small amounts of tasteful morsels like nuts, seeds, olives, or dried cranberries, but not all at once. I particularly like pine nuts, walnuts, sunflower seeds, and avocado.

- Avoid white foods like sugar, flour, bread, rice, and potatoes. Choose whole-wheat or multi-grain products of flour, cereal, pasta, or bread. Try Pepperidge Farms® light bread of 45 calories per slice or Thomas'® light multi-grain English muffin (100 calories). Use whole-wheat mini pita bread, or even better the kind like Joseph's that also contains flax and oat bran. Choose brown rice and sweet potatoes. Use sugar substitutes in moderation. Try Truvia™, "Nature's Calorie-Free Sweetener" or consider less sweetener completely.
- Prepare skinless chicken breast in a wide variety of preparations using taste-enhancing seasonings and condiments, appropriate for Italian (basil and oregano), Southwest (ground chili pepper and cumin), or Asian flavors (light soy sauce and ground ginger). Grill salmon often. Make sure foods stay moist. Nothing is worse than dried up chicken or fish. Ask my husband! Minimize red meat consumption.
- Eat lots of fruit. I love berries and melons and still believe the urban myth that grapefruit citrus cancels its calories altogether. Eat lots of vegetables, raw, steamed, or microwaved. Adorn with minimum of salt or olive oil. Rub corn-on-the-cob with lime.
- What to eat when I'm hungry and it's not mealtime: clementines, apples, mini-carrots (count out 6 at a time),

hummus (not the whole container), almonds (count out 6 at a time and put the bag away), sugar-free Jell-O®.

- Beverage choices: I must start the day with rich strong coffee (my favorite is Starbucks Sumatra) with fat-free milk but no sweetener. (I cannot be on a diet that instructs me to give up caffeine.) I love flavored sparkling water with no calories or artificial sweeteners from Poland Springs and Polar. In chilly weather, I drink hot tea, either traditional or flavored herbal. Nestlé fat-free hot cocoa mix is a special treat (each packet is only 25 calories).
- When the weather is warm, I make sun tea by putting 5 tea bags in a half-gallon clear bottle or pitcher and leave in the sun for a couple of hours, then refrigerate and add lemon when drinking. It's not bitter from boiling, so no sweetener is needed. I also adore iced diet tonic water with lime (tastes just like a real cocktail without any calories).
- And speaking of cocktails, minimize alcohol intake—a tough one for me. I love wine, so when seriously dieting I limit wine to accompanying special meals or on special occasions. Start drinking later in the evening, and try to alternate with sparkling water. Sometimes I just have a one-ounce nightcap of a favorite liqueur.
- Special treats: a small piece of dark chocolate; frozen low-fat yogurt, just half-cup in a small bowl (my favorite is Brigham's élan black raspberry); Dove bar miniature ice cream treats (70 calories each, but just eat one!)

Acknowledgments

My four decades of canine ownership experiences have essentially evolved while dog parenting in tandem with my husband Jesse Jupiter. Dog ownership has always been our joint effort, from the time we brought our first rusty Irish setter puppy home to upend our Arizona life to currently sharing our suburban Boston habitat with two diurnally active English springer spaniels who proprietarily sprawl in our marital bed by night. I immensely appreciate the time and energy Jesse has devoted to our sporty dogs, as well as his constant and unwavering love and support for me throughout our life together.

I am also inspired by Jesse's tireless dedication to his work as an orthopaedic surgeon, which is evident in his myriad of accomplishments, grateful patients, and admiring medical colleagues. Similarly, the creative dedication of our daughter Stacy Jupiter to her work as a marine biologist, coral reef conservationist, writer, and artist has also inspired me in my own creative pursuits.

From childhood into adulthood, I was fortunate to have continuous love and support from my parents Rita and Morton Abrams. Sadly, they will not be able to take pride in my first book, as my father is deceased and my mother is not well. I also appreciated the motivational encouragement of my uncle Arthur Sherman. He was always one of my greatest writing boosters, but has also sadly passed on before I could share my accomplishment with him.

In addition to living with our six sporty canines, I also observed and learned much from beloved pet dogs of many breeds that belonged to close family and friends. Most were referenced at some point in my book, but I would also like to acknowledge them here as well as mention a few more. Many dogs have been integral parts of our extended family: my parents' shih tzu Shanghai; my mother's papillon Foxy; my sister Carol Gart's family sheltie Shelby; the Kaplans' Rhodesian ridgebacks Vicky, Rocky, and Sammy; the Spetalnicks' West Highland terrier Maxie; cousin Claudia Jupiter Merson's canine succession of Dalmatian Ruby, yellow Labrador Donna, and black Lab mix Sophie; our son Ben Jupiter's golden retriever Loki; and my niece Marissa Gart's shar-pei/beagle mix Hank.

Similarly, many of my friends have owned precious pets that have enhanced their family lives: the Goodmans and their standard poodles Boomer and Riggs; the Hastings and their Portuguese water dogs Galli, Nikki, and Cinco; the Driscolls and their keeshonds Smokey and Bandit; the Belskys and their white standard poodles; the Cubells and their English cocker spaniels Zack and Kobi; and Susan Tofias and her Airedale terrier Casey.

Furthermore, I have certainly appreciated the many other friends and family members who have enjoyed my various articles over the years and highly encouraged me to write an entire book. So finally, I did! And I extend my thanks to all of you who spurred me on.

About the Author

Dr. Beryl Jupiter is a published reporter, columnist, and feature storywriter, predominantly for community newspapers in the Boston area. Before writing professionally, she began a career path in psychology, earning a bachelor's degree from the University of Pennsylvania and a doctoral degree from Boston University. Her psychology work primarily involved teaching at various colleges while simultaneously managing a domestic household for her indefatigable surgeon husband, their two children, and usually two dogs at any given time. Currently Dr. Jupiter continues to apply many psychology principles in the socialization of the family dogs.

Facebook page: The Puppy Diet
puppydiet@gmail.com

Made in the USA
Columbia, SC
09 March 2023